What is This Thing Called

FAITH?

Meditations with Reflections on the Sayings of Jesus

Hugh Duffy, Ph.D

Lanalea Media LLC

Riviera Beach, Florida

First Published by Lanalea Media, LLC
4050 Dorado Drive
Riviera Beach, Florida 33418
www.LanaleaMedia.com

Publisher's Note: This is a devotional book. Locales and public names are sometimes used for illustrative purposes. The quotations used in this book are taken from *The New American Bible* © 1987 by World Bible Publishers, Inc.

Book Layout © 2015 BookDesignTemplates.com. Modifications, additions and cover design by Richard W. Grigonis. Cover photo © djgis / Shutterstock.

What is This Thing Called Faith? Meditations with Reflections on the Sayings of Jesus / Hugh Duffy – 1st Edition.

ISBN: 978-0-692-53926-2

DEDICATION

to

"Those who hear the word of God and keep it."

—Luke 11:28

This is a meditational book for all those who strive to appreciate God's Word in Scripture.

Contents

ACKNOWLEDGEMENTS

There are several people without whom I could not have written this book. Richard William Grigonis, my faithful editor, has been an indispensable help in putting this book together.

Michael and Kay Bartlett have made a most valuable contribution to this book by assembling and copying all of the meditations and articles I published in various parish bulletins on this topic during the course of my 30 years as pastor of Sacred Heart Catholic Church, Okeechobee, Florida.

Dr. Anne Boyes and Cathleen Blair devoted endless hours not only to proofread the manuscript but also by their addition of valuable suggestions for the improvement of the book.

Alvaro Ortega, my webmaster at FatherDuffy.com did a masterful job in organizing and categorizing my many meditations on the website.

I would like to offer a general word of thanks to all the amazing people, too numerous to mention, who have influenced and inspired me over the years in the various parishes where I have been assigned to write this book. Their influence, though invisible in the pages of this book, was a strong force in bringing this work to completion.

No man is an island and we are all part of the main. This book is a product of several interconnecting relationships that have occurred throughout my life, beginning with my family upbringing in Ireland and continuing through my seminary experience, my university days in Dublin, Ireland, University of Poitier in France, Harvard University in Cambridge, Massachusetts, and the University of Hull where I obtained my Ph.D. All of these comprise the foundational sources of my spiritual and intellectual development.

I would be remiss if I did not thank the Lord, the benefactor of this gracious gift of faith, for which I am so privileged to possess in spite of human weakness.

Faith is marvelous gift; it is like a precious diamond that is multi-faceted and ever-new in its manifestations. Though faith is constantly new and transformative, it always remains the same because it derives from the One God who created us. Each one of us can never give expression to the totality of this great mystery of faith. We can only, at best, offer a partial glimpse or appreciation of this gift as we meditate on His Word and practice it.

FOREWORD

I met Father Hugh Duffy through a set of circumstances that could only be termed providential. Although our homes are only a few blocks from each other, we had never met or known of each other until about a year ago when we were introduced by a mutual friend. Although we are from different denominations (Roman Catholic and Protestant) and different vocations (Priest and Christian counselor/educator), we became immediate friends because of our shared commitment to Christ. Since that time we have spent many happy hours together discussing the things of God. During those conversations I have come to view him as one of the most kind and Godly men I have ever known, and I believe, as you read the pages of this book of meditations, even if you never meet Father Duffy in person on this earth, you will experience his kindness and Godliness through the pages of this book.

God's Word encourages us to study the Scriptures so we can understand them correctly (2 Timothy 2:15, 3:16–17). This is particularly true for theological scholars and pastors who teach us the Word each week. But there is something that God encourages us all to do much more frequently than academic theological study itself, and that is the activity of biblical meditation.

Biblical Meditation

The word "meditation" has been largely conscripted in the twenty-first century by those who believe it involves sitting in the lotus position, emptying our minds of conscious thoughts and chanting repeated Tibetan phrases such as the mantra "OM."

In contrast, biblical meditation is very different. Instead of emptying our minds we focus our minds on a specific passage of Scripture, take time to fully understand it in its context, and then ask God to help us understand how He wants us to use that truth in our thinking and daily lives. Father Duffy's book of meditations and reflections does precisely this.

Many hundreds of Scriptures encourage us to spend time each day in meditation. Here is the reason I believe it does so: Our love for Scripture reflects our love for God and our desire to be in relationship with Him.

Father Duffy's book encourages us, if we are not already doing so, to develop the habit of taking a few minutes each day to read a passage of Scripture, meditate on its meaning, and then ask God how He wants us to apply it in our lives.

One of the foremost advocates of meditation was King David who, significantly, was called "a man after God's own heart." If we want to be known likewise, we may want to adopt the same attitude toward the Scriptures as King David did.

Psalm 119 offers one of the most beautiful meditations in the entire Bible: "May the words of my mouth and the meditation of my heart be pleasing in Your sight, Oh Lord, my Rock and Redeemer" (Psalm 119:14).

"I have hidden Your Word in my heart that I might not sin against you" (Psalm 119:2).

"Your Word is a lamp to my feet and a light to my paths" (Psalm 119:105).

In the New Testament, the importance of meditation is highlighted by the words of Mary, the mother of Jesus, regarding her son's mission: "Mary treasured all these things and pondered them in her heart" (Luke 2:19).

The Canticle of Mary in Luke 1:46–55 begins with
"My soul magnifies the Lord,
And my spirit rejoices in God my savior."

This canticle, also called the Magnificat, is one of the most treasured meditations in all of the New Testament.

The opening chapter of St. John's gospel (John 1:1) which begins "In the beginning was the Word, and the Word was God" offers a profound meditation on the mystery of the Incarnation.

Gerald Manley Hopkins, a Catholic poet who was much influenced by George Herbert, a Protestant poet, wrote:

"Christ plays in ten thousand places.

lovely in limbs, and lovely in eyes not his,

to the Father through the features of men's faces."

This book by Father Duffy deals with the richness of the gift of Faith. He draws on the powerful Faith of Christ as seen throughout a variety of contexts, places and faces.

We experience the living faith of people like the Samaritan leper; St. Peter; Mary Magdalene; Zacchaeus the tax collector; the backsliding-doubting-Thomas; the blind man; the woman who suffered from hemorrhages; the Canaanite woman; the pagan centurion; and the magnificent faith of Mary, the mother of Jesus.

These personal meditations are offered as a springboard for the reader's own reflections, and as a means of applying them to the reader's own personal life. What is also interesting about the book is that each meditation and reflection is complimented and rounded off by an appropriate prayer.

A social psychology experiment done during the days of World War II gives us, I believe, a hint of why biblical meditation can be such an important part of our Christian lives. There was a shortage of meat available during the war years, and there was a need to have mothers and families cook and use some of the cuts of meat that people weren't using regularly, such as kidneys, tongue, etc.

A research study was designed to see which of two methods would be more effective in motivating mothers and families to use some of these portions. Women were randomly divided into two groups. One group heard lectures from a professional nutritionist on how to tastefully prepare these cuts of meat. The other group was a discussion group in which homemakers and mothers brainstormed ways to prepare and serve these cuts of meat. The ideas were generated by the participants themselves

The researchers then did a follow-up study to see which group of women actually started using the cuts of meat that had been either presented by an expert lecturer or that were the result of the women's own discussion. They found that the women who had come up with applications using the ideas themselves were much more likely to use these ideas in their own families.

How does this research study apply to the material in this book? It certainly does not mean to stop attending church and listening to sermons presented by pastors, for God tells us to "not give up meeting together as some are in the habit of doing, but let us encourage one another—and all the more as you see the Day approaching" (Hebrews 10:25). We all need the encouragement that comes from gathering with other believers to worship and hear the Word. But to really grow in our Christian lives—to have the Word make changes in our Christian lives on Monday through Saturday—we need to be engaged in the activity encouraged in this book—personally reading the Word and asking God how He wants us to use its truth to change our lives.

And that is how I encourage you to use this book of meditations and reflections by Father Duffy. Read one devotion a day, then spend a few moments in meditation and prayer, asking God how He wants you to apply that truth in your own life.

Prof. Henry Virkler, Ph.D
Professor of Counseling
Palm Beach Atlantic University

INTRODUCTION

This book is the first of a trilogy about Faith, Hope, and Love. For the believer, these three virtues are essential in order to live a Christ-like life. They are called theological virtues because, unlike the moral and cardinal virtues (Prudence, Justice, Temperance, and Fortitude) that can be taught and practiced by anyone; Faith, Hope, and Love are gifts of grace from God Himself. They are the very foundation of the Christian life, and as such they give life to all the other moral virtues; they are the pledge of the presence of the Holy Spirit acting in and through the lives of devout Christians.

The three theological virtues, Faith, Hope, and Love, have different functions in the lives of Christians. Hence, Faith can be viewed as the root; Hope as the shoot; and Love as the fruit of a grace-filled life. Notwithstanding their different functions, these three theological virtues are also interconnected; they cannot really be separated from each other. Faith without the good works of Love is dead (James 2:17). Hope without Faith and Love would be barren for Hope sustains the other two by imparting the power to refrain from despair and to never give up. The virtue of Hope relates to the aspiration of happiness which God has placed in every human heart, not just as something to be achieved in this life but also in the next (Colossians 1:27). Love, the greatest of the three (1 Corinthians 13:13), can only be fruitful when it is grounded on faith in God's Revelation and on the hope in His promises (Romans 1:5:16:25).

There are many books written on the three theological virtues. Pope Benedict XVI, for example, has written encyclicals on each of them: 'Lumen fidei' on Faith, 'Spe Salvi' on Hope, and 'Deus Caritas est' on Love. Lumen Fidei, however, was written in conjunction with Pope Francis.

So, why one may ask would I find it necessary to write another book or books on the subject of the theological virtues? The answer is really pastoral; that is, it addresses the need to enable today's Christians to have a personal appreciation of Faith, Hope and Love in the scriptures, and to respond to them wholeheartedly in their lives. This is the pastoral challenge that this first book on Faith endeavors to address since the gift of the Holy Spirit is given to all baptized Christians who possess the right and privilege to open themselves up to the word of God in scripture and to put it into practice (Luke 11:28).

I have been studying and writing about this subject for many years. In 2004, I published my Ph.D on the relationship between faith and reason under the title: Queen of the Sciences. Since then, I have discovered that there are a lot of inquiring Christians out there who are very interested in gaining a deeper scriptural appreciation of their faith, and how it relates to their lives. During thirty years of service as a pastor in Florida, I have written extensively on this topic in parish bulletins and other publications. Several of my parishioners suggested that I should start a website to reach more people so that they and others like them could read my messages. I took their advice and started a website: www.fatherduffy.com. My website audience has grown to over three million visitors since its inception in 2010.

Several readers have constantly urged me to publish these meditations in a book. After reflection and consultation I decided to publish three books, devoted to each of the three theological virtues. It also occurred to me that I should include an interactive section of reflections along with each scriptural meditation.

This first book is an integral unit of fifty meditations and reflections on the theological virtue of faith.

There are other pastoral reasons for writing this book. Ever since the Second Vatican Council (1960–1965) the Catholic faithful have been paying more attention to the scriptures than they were accustomed to in the past when they were dissuaded from reading the scriptures. The church's dogmatic constitution on Divine Revelation has restored the scriptures to its proper place in the spiritual lives of the faithful, stating that "Access to Sacred Scripture ought to be open wide to the Christian faithful" and it quotes St. Jerome, the great scripture scholar, who said that "Ignorance of the scriptures is ignorance of Christ" (Vatican II, Dei Verbum, Chapter VI, no. 22 and no. 25).

Nowhere is the importance of the scriptures more evident among the Catholic faithful, in a practical way, than in the Church's liturgy. The church's celebration of the Mass has readings from both the Old and New Testaments; homilies are focused on the scriptures; and lay lectors proclaim the living word during the liturgy. This renewed emphasis on scripture, however, doesn't stop here. The new Catechism of the Catholic Church is also remarkable in that it contains constant references from scripture in support of its teaching. Things have come a long way, as far as the Catholic emphasis on scripture is concerned, when an American televangelist, Jack Van Impe, has delivered commentaries on the Catholic Catechism because he appreciated that it was immersed in Scripture.

I would be remiss if I did not mention Pope Francis as an example of someone who listens to the Word of God in Scripture and practices it. Pope Francis, it has been remarked, is a Christ-centered person. His talks, his writings, and his actions have universal appeal because they are permeated with the Good News of the Gospel. He is known to urge people to carry a small version of the New Testament with them on their person so that they can meditate on it frequently.

Why This Book?

This book offers answers and a hands-on experience of the faith for people today because it is based on the sayings of Jesus in Scripture. In spite of the renewed emphasis on scripture, there is unfortunately a falling away today of Christians from the practice of the faith. Young people are abandoning mainline churches and they are left to wander about like ships without a rudder in today's cruel world. I've witnessed this in parishes all over the country where I have been an Outreach Speaker for Cross International. Knowledge of the faith for many young people today is minimal and in some cases almost nonexistent. It is not that people don't care; it is just that they are not motivated or excited about faith in their lives. As an educator I know how important motivation is. I also know how important it was to Jesus who says: "I have come to set the earth on fire and how I wish it were ignited" (Luke 12:49). Faith is like a fire within, and it has to be lived passionately with conviction. John Henry Cardinal Newman in the *Grammar of Ascent* described Faith as an "illative sense," a sort of sixth sense, an intuition or gift we are privileged to possess.

Faith should not be identified strictly with beliefs because faith is a special spiritual quality or gift bestowed upon the person. Such was the case with the Centurion in the gospel who, although he was a pagan, was rewarded for his faith (Luke 1–10). The same can be said of the Canaanite woman who Jesus healed (Matthew 15:21–28) and the Samaritan woman at the well (John 4:1–26) in whose village He spent several days.

We must never forget that faith is a gift. We do not merit it for it is given freely to people of goodwill by the Holy Spirit which, as Scripture says: "goes where it wills" (John 3:8).

The gift of faith cannot be imposed on us (by any human authority) but we can dispose ourselves to accept it when we open our hearts in love to the living Word of God in Scripture.

Although well-meaning, Christians sometimes make the mistake of confusing the gift of faith with beliefs or doctrines and, in their zeal to save others, they try to force their beliefs on them. This can have disastrous consequences, and I have encountered many instances where this has badly affected people.

I was walking in the parking lot of the church where I served as pastor in Okeechobee, Florida, while another priest was celebrating

Mass. It was a typical sun-drenched morning in Florida, so I had to keep my exercise brief. A man was making his way towards me from the opposite direction, and we stopped to talk.

He told me he was killing time and was waiting for his wife who was singing in the choir. I remarked that I had observed him on other occasions pacing the parking lot during Mass time, and I was curious to know why he didn't attend Church himself.

"I got turned off from religion in my youth, and have never set foot inside a church ever since," he said, shaking his head dismissively.

"What happened, if you don't mind me asking?" I continued.

"My father was a minister, and he used to force me to accept his beliefs by dunking my head into a pail of water whenever I couldn't recite exactly what he told me. That's why I gave up on religion and don't go to church," he concluded.

As I was walking away, I realized that this unfortunate man had been abused by his preacher father who, in his zeal, tried to impose his beliefs onto his son. By forcing his beliefs on his son, the father effectively prevented him from enjoying the gift of faith, which God alone can give. Faith is a gift, and we should never play God by thinking we are the purveyors of this gift. The best we can do is be examples of this gift to others.

In this particular book, I will be dealing with the Christian Faith specifically. Newman also makes an important distinction between a notional faith and a real faith. A notional faith has to do with the acceptance of doctrinal propositions such as we find in the Christian Creed and in the church's teachings. There's nothing wrong with that in itself but it is not enough. A real faith is based on a personal response to the living word of the Gospel; it is a heartfelt faith because it is rooted in an encounter with Christ. In other words, it is personal knowledge or the wisdom that comes from personal experience.

There is always a need for a fresh approach to old truths if Christians want to remain relevant in today's world. The truths of Faith are ancient, but they are forever new (The Confessions of St. Augustine:

Book X). This modest book on Faith, I feel, serves an urgent pastoral need (by pastoral I mean personal and practical) in that it addresses the subject of faith in the language of people today.

The remarkable thing about Jesus's sayings is that they are so simple, yet so profound. He spoke with authority (Matthew 7:29) about deep issues of the soul to the ordinary people of His day in language and stories they could easily understand.

It is in this spirit that I endeavor to convey the message of salvation; that is, in simple language, using story and images from contemporary life.

How to Use This Book

As I've already said, this book consists of fifty meditations, followed by reflections, on the sayings of Jesus. These sayings, which I've chosen, are by no means exhaustive. They are intended to provide the reader with pertinent examples of what Jesus had to say about faith. The scriptural mediations in the book sometimes include Old Testament readings because Jesus is the fulfilment of the Old Testament (Matthew 5:17), and are intended to awaken the readers appreciation of the gift of faith.

Since the Holy Spirt is given for the benefit of everyone (John 3:8), the reader is given an opportunity to share his or her experience of faith under the guidance of the Holy Spirit. The opportunity to appropriate the message personally by each individual is offered in the reflections which follow each meditation.

Each meditation is headed by a verse of Scripture. It is recommended, before engaging in the reflections; that the readers become acquainted with the scriptural verse in context in order to better understand the message. This would mean having a Bible available to look up and read the entire scripture passage. This is not absolutely necessary, but it would be helpful. Fortified with this prior knowledge, the reader will then be able to engage in the reflections with more depth and insight.

The questions posed in the reflections address the main points of each meditation. Again, these questions are not exhaustive (the reader might have other questions as well) because the Holy Spirit is the ultimate guide and, as Jesus assures us, the Holy Spirit brings us to a fuller understanding of his word (John 14:26).

The Bible is our text, but the Holy Spirit is our guide. Anyone with an open mind can benefit from this book which is offered as an aid to meditation, the kind of scriptural meditation which Professor Henry Virkler described so well in the Foreword to this book.

This particular book could well be described as a meditational book. The importance of meditation cannot be overemphasized for it is an essential spiritual activity. This was impressed on me one day when I had a positive encounter with another man in the parking lot of the church where I worked.

The door of his car was wide open and, thinking he was having a problem, I approached his car and asked if he needed help.

He looked up at me and said he was reading his Bible which he was gently holding in his lap. I complimented him and asked him how long he had been doing this; namely, meditating on the Bible.

With tears in his eyes, he told me he was doing this most of his adult life. He had been injured in World War II and, when in hospital, he found a Bible in the table by his bed. It was a Gideon Bible and "I began reading it," he told me. It was, he said; "the best medicine I ever received, and slowly it restored me to health. I read it now every day," he continued. "I always carry a dictionary with me so I can look up big words, but the Holy Spirit is my teacher and he never lets me down."

This self-effacing man, whom I was blessed to encounter, understood well the importance of meditating on the scriptures. And this is why I have written this book.

At the end of each reflection in this book, there is a prayer, chosen according to the message, to elicit one's faith. This prayer is a valuable way of connecting with the Lord in the privacy of one's heart.

Fr. Hugh Duffy, Ph.D
Riviera Beach, Florida
May 2016

What is This Thing Called
FAITH?

[1] Faith and Family

"They took the child up to Jerusalem to be presented in the Temple."

—The Gospel of Luke, chapter 2:22

A social researcher was conducting a study of an Amish village. The Amish live in traditional rural villages in America far from industrialization and technology. They have no computers, televisions, refrigerators or telephones inside their homes. In his study of the Amish village school, the researcher noticed that the children never screamed or yelled. This surprised him, so he decided to check it out with the teacher. He told the teacher that he had not once heard an Amish child yell, and asked him why that was so? The teacher replied, "Have you ever heard any Amish parent yell?" The message was clear: Like parents, like children.

In Luke 2:22 we read about the parents of Jesus who make the long journey to Jerusalem to present their firstborn child in the Temple as the Law of Moses required. In the image of Joseph and Mary presenting Jesus in the Temple, we have a wonderful model of a family united in practicing the faith and in raising their child in the faith.

We read that "When the time came for their purification according to the Law of Moses, they brought him up to Jerusalem to present him to the Lord" (Luke 2:22). Joseph and Mary are presented as people who keep God's laws. Moreover, they are presented as doing it as a family. It is easier to walk in the ways of God when husband and wife walk it together with their children and encourage each other along the way. The book of Ecclesiastes says: "Two are better than one, because they have a good return for their work: If one falls down, the other can help him up. But pity the man who falls down and has no one to help him up!" (Ecclesiastes 4:9–10). Joseph and Mary are companions in the journey of life, but especially in their journey of faith.

Some people wonder why the baby Jesus, who was not in a position to say yes or no, should be initiated into the Jewish religion without his consent? This is a problem also for those who question the value of infant baptism. They feel that baptism has no value until a child reaches the age of reason and then is able to decide for oneself. But this is not the example that Mary and Joseph are giving in Luke, chapter 2. The criticism about Jesus' presentation in the Temple, like the criticism about the value of infant baptism, is born out of an exaggerated individualism in modern society. In the Biblical era, people saw the whole family as one. The question of husband, wife and child acting independently was unthinkable. Thus we hear in the Acts of the Apostles that when certain men and women were converted, they were baptized together with their entire household (Acts 16:15, 31; 18:18).

If parents are to provide their children with the basic necessities of life, what is more basic than one's faith in God? It is true that faith is a gift, and only God offers us that gift. We don't merit it for it is God's gift to us. But, the gift of faith can be nurtured in us through the example of those who possess it. That is why the example of parents is so vital in the upbringing of children. No parent would think of allowing their children to decide whether they want to go to school or not; whether they want to learn the same language or not; whether they want to be a citizen of their country or not. These decisions are made for them, knowing very well that when they grow up, they may decide to follow a different path. This family unity is what we see today in the example of Joseph and Mary who presented Jesus in the Jewish Temple.

The example of Joseph and Mary, and the example of the Amish community, show that the best way to nurture the gift of faith in children is not by shouting at them but by showing them what faith means in your life. If this was good enough for the parents of Jesus, it should be good enough for us.

Reflection:

"They took the child up to Jerusalem to be presented in the Temple."

To better understand the above scriptural verse in context, you will find it helpful to read the entire passage: Luke 2:22–32.

Please reflect on the following:

1. What is the significance for you of the Presentation of Jesus in the Temple?

   _____

   _____

2. How does the support of family nurture the gift of faith?

   Give examples:

   _____

   _____

3. Would you say the example of parents is vital in the growth of a child's faith? If so, why?

   _____

   Give examples:

   _____

   _____

4. Prayer:

> Lord Jesus, You have told us
> That unless we become like little children
> We shall not enter into Your kingdom.
> Bless all families and the children of the world
> With Your faith and vision so as to recognize
> We are all God's children, created in His likeness.

[2] Faith and Fear

"Be not afraid, but believe."

—*The Gospel of Mark*, chapter 5:36

This scripture adds a new twist to the old saying, "where there's life, there's hope." For the Christian, it seems truer to say, "Where there's faith there's life." If we are looking for signs of life in a given situation, then we must first look for signs of faith. For faith leads to life as we can see in chapter five of St. Mark's Gospel, where the faith of a synagogue official and the woman who suffered from a hemorrhage were rewarded with New Life.

Biblical literature looks upon death not so much as the antithesis of life but as a part of life. Life is God's gift. Death is the end of our mortal lives, and the entry into eternal life.

Scripture also reminds us that we are made "imperishable," in the "image of" God's "own nature." The Gospel of St. Mark, chapter five, deftly presents vivid examples of new life and, at the same time, links new life to the faith the people had in Jesus.

This scripture has reference, not only to the faith of an unnamed woman and a small-time synagogue official, named Jairus. Veiled in the story is the powerful faith of Jesus Himself. Jesus' faith in His Father and in His own mission underlies today's Scripture. He does not hesitate when confronted by Jairus' request. Jesus has faith and pursues it. When touched by the woman with the hemorrhage, Jesus shares His faith with her. He heals her. When He reaches the lifeless daughter of the official, He gives her life.

Jesus' faith withstands and overcomes all the disbelief He encounters. His faith is a model for our own. Life, regrettably, is often filled with doomsayers. Jesus shows us the meaning and the necessity of grounding ourselves in faith. So grounded, we can, like Jesus, remain faithful and become life-givers.

Often we feel that our faith is too weak, too filled with questions, and never pure enough. Such weakness makes us afraid of faith. But seeking, questioning, and asking God are all parts of faith. The God of life is revealed even in our feeblest attempts to live faith-filled lives.

That is why Jesus says: "Be not afraid, but believe."

Reflection:

"Be not afraid, but believe."

To better understand the above scriptural verse in context, you will find it helpful to read the entire passage: Mark 5:21–43.

Please reflect on the following:

1. The faith of Jesus in Mark 5:21–43 overcame the disbelief of all naysayers, including His disciples.

   Do you call on Him like the synagogue official and the woman with the hemorrhage?

   Give examples in your personal life of the Lord's healing.

   _____

   _____

2. How does the Bible look upon death? Is it the antithesis of life or is it an integral part of life?

   _____

   _____

   How do you feel about death? Your answer to this question will have a bearing on how you live.

   _____

   _____

3. What was the secret to the healing of the synagogue official and the woman with the hemorrhage?

_____

_____

4. Prayer:

> Let nothing disturb you,
> Nothing frighten you,
> All things are passing,
> God alone never changes.
> Patience endures all things.
> Whoever has God lacks for nothing.
> He alone is enough.
>
> —St. Teresa of Avila, 1515–1582

[3] Faith and Doubt

"My Lord and My God"

—*The Gospel of John*, chapter 20

At times we feel that life has put us through the rinse cycle. This is how St. Thomas felt after the crucifixion of Jesus. His life had fallen apart and, even though he heard stories about the Lord's Resurrection, his mind was wracked with doubt. He wanted to experience the risen Lord, to put his hand into His side, before committing himself to this new found faith in the resurrection.

When Thomas saw that the risen Lord was really worth believing in, he exclaimed: "My Lord and My God." This exclamation of Thomas is one of the greatest professions of faith in the Gospels.

It has been said that those who begin with certitude end with doubt, and those who begin with doubt end with certitude. Thomas began with doubt about the Resurrection of Jesus and ended with certitude, a certitude that burst forth into his shout of faith: "My Lord and My God."

We have not seen with our eyes the risen Lord that Thomas touched with his hands. We are among those who have not seen but believe. We believe, in spite of doubt, because we can experience the risen Lord in our own lives and in the lives of those who strive to follow his example.

I was giving a sermon recently at a church in Decatur, Illinois, and I was explaining how important it was to experience the risen Christ as something real and present in our lives right now. I mentioned that Christians, generally, can accept the Resurrection of Christ as a historical event or their own resurrection "at the last day" (John 11:24).

But acceptance of this new life of the Resurrection right now, in your own life, is not as easy to accept. While I was talking in this vein, a man in the pew raised his hand and offered this testimony:

"I'm glad to hear you say this, for I had stage four cancer and was given no hope of survival. I gave my life over to the Lord the way you said, and my life changed completely. When I went to see the doctor, the cancer was totally gone. I never expected this and the doctor couldn't make sense of it. I went about my life with a new spirit and with more joy than I ever had experienced. On weekends, I am now able to sing karaoke with my friends at our local rendezvous."

When the man finished saying this, the congregation burst into spontaneous applause. This man got a new lease on life because he had accepted the promise of Christ that He is "the Resurrection and the Life" (John 11:25).

When we say, "I believe," we are taking a stand. We are embarking on a journey, a journey of faith that is well worth the effort. "Do not persist in your unbelief, but believe," says the Lord (John: 20:27)/

Few can accept this crisp command but to those who can accept, it is eye-opening. It is worthy of the shout of faith:

"My Lord and My God."

Reflection:

"My Lord and My God"

To better understand the above scriptural verse in context, you will find it helpful to read the entire passage: John: 24–28.

Please reflect on the following:

1. Is doubt compatible with faith?

_____

_____

Give an example of a Saint who struggled with doubt.

_____

_____

Give examples of some beliefs you hold in spite of doubt.

_____

_____

2. What is the significance of St. Thomas' profession of faith?

_____

_____

3. The Lord says: "Blessed are they who have not seen but believe." Who is the Lord referring to here?

_____

_____

4. Prayer:

> To you I call, O God,
> For You will surely heed me.
> Turn your ear to me,
> Hear my feeble words,
> Guard me as the apple of Your eye,
> And, in the shadow of Your wings,
> Protect me.

[4] Faith and Evil

"The fool says in his heart, there is no God."

—*Psalm* 14:1

Sometimes we encounter someone who, seemingly, has no faith, but when that person is put in a worship situation he/she can be moved to tears. What is the reason for this? Why would a person of no faith be moved by someone of faith? Jean Jacques Rousseau, the great French philosopher, was an unbeliever, but he was moved to tears by the faith of his wife who was a devout Catholic.

Rabbi Marc Gellman, writing for a newspaper column, titled: *The God Squad* received a letter from a man, an acknowledged unbeliever, who wrote: "Whenever I go into Church, I begin to weep immediately and sometimes can't stop. Is this guilt and shame of having no faith?"

The Rabbi wrote back: "My best advice to you is to try to understand more deeply the meaning of your tears. My suspicion is that your tears and your doubts are the result of a kind of spiritual paralysis in the face of the great contradiction between an evil world and a good God."

People are easily torn between the goodness of God and the evil of the world. It is like the story of the postman who was delivering mail to a house when suddenly he was confronted by a growling dog preventing his entry to the home. The owner of the house appeared at the door, and shouted to the mailman:

"Pay no attention to the dog's growl; he won't touch you. Look at his tail: it's wagging."

"That's my problem, said the policeman. I don't know which end to believe."

Which is best to believe: a loving God or an unloving world? Scripture tells us that "God so loved the world He sent His only son that whoever believes in Him might not perish but have everlasting life" (John 3:17). The world is not a bad place if we approach it with the right attitude. The goodness of God can shine through the wonders of Creation; the birth of a child; the beauty of people who are touched by compassion, generosity, forgiveness, faith, hope and love. This is the right stuff which is the antithesis to a world gone badly wrong through selfish ambition and greed. The depths of evil in the world have been overcome through the crucifixion and resurrection of Jesus which spurs us to reject the abjectness of an evil world and embrace the goodness of the Lord. We have a choice. Which will it be? Accept a loving God or accept an unloving world without God.

This is why Scripture states: "The fool says in his heart, there is no God."

Reflection:

"The fool says in his heart, there is no God."

To better understand the above scriptural verse in context, you will find it helpful to read the entire passage: Psalm 14:1–7.
Please reflect on the following:

1. Why is it foolish to say, there is no God?

    _____

    _____

    What examples can you give from your experience of the goodness of the Lord?

    _____

    _____

2. What are some obstacles in life to belief in God's goodness? Give examples:

    _____

    _____

3. What is your response to the existence of evil?

    _____

    _____

Where would you find a solution?

_____

_____

4. Prayer:

There is none that can resist
The will of the Lord,
For You have made all things:
The heaven and the earth,
And all that is held within
The circle of life.

[5] Faith and Healing

"I have not found such faith in Israel."

—*The Gospel of Matthew*, chapter 8:10

When Jesus entered Capernaum, a centurion approached Him to ask His help, "Sir, my servant lies sick at home. He is paralyzed and suffers terribly." Jesus said to him, "I will come and heal him." The centurion answered, "I am not worthy to have you under my roof. Just give an order and my boy will be healed. When Jesus heard this He was astonished and said to those who were following Him, "I tell you, I have not found such faith in Israel" (Matthew 8:5–10).

The centurion was certainly a pagan, an officer in the Roman military. He was clearly a man of good will. Yet this foreigner; this pagan; had the gift of faith, and he believed in Jesus who could cure his servant of his "dreadful suffering." What's more, the centurion was willing to expose himself to the censure of his superiors and to the back-biting of his associates and subordinates by humbly asking Jesus to cure his servant. Jesus held up this man's faith as an example to all of us.

Everyone is in need of Jesus' healing touch whether it is physical, psychological, emotional, or spiritual. The Centurion is a confident example of faith in Jesus who, over and over again, instructs us to 'ask,' 'knock,' 'seek' and 'find' whatever it is we need. The Lord may not answer our prayers the way we expect them to be answered, but he will answer them the way we need to have them answered. His response to our prayers may turn a difficult situation into a healing one or it may move us to be more compassionate towards others. God's ways are not our ways, but whether we realize it or not, He will reward us for our faith because He is a good and generous God.

Has Jesus found faith like this in you? Now is the time for strengthening your own faith. This is a good time to renew your trust in Jesus like the centurion who was not afraid to take risks. Life is a risk, but so is faith! Have you faith that God will watch over you in spite of the problems and difficulties you encounter in life? This is the faith that makes a way through the mountains and the valleys in your life.

The faith of the Centurion is such an important symbol for the Church that his response to Jesus: "I am not worthy to have you enter under my roof" is recited by every Catholic before reception of the Eucharist at every Mass.

Reflection:

"I have not found such faith in Israel."

To better understand the above scriptural verse in context, you will find it helpful to read the entire passage: Matthew 8:5–13.
Please reflect on the following:

1. What does the pagan Centurion illustrate about the gift of faith?

_____

_____

2. Is faith open to all people of good will?

_____

_____

3. Why is the Centurion's faith an inspiration for all of us?

_____

_____

4. How does your faith help you with life's problems?

Give examples.

_____

_____

5. Prayer:

> Lord, make me deserving of the gift of faith
> Forgive my shortcomings; show me your way.
> Endow me with courage to resist temptation.
> Protect me from the envy of others,
> And from my own selfishness,
> So as to serve You, and never be parted from you.

[6] Faith and Sight

"One thing I do know: I was blind, and now I see."

—*The Gospel of John*, chapter 9:25

Chapter nine of St. John's Gospel tells the story of Jesus curing a blind man of his blindness. The blind man is not the only blind person in the story. The Pharisees who resented Jesus for curing the blind man on the Sabbath were just as blind, but they didn't know it. What about you? This is what you need to consider.

We can see "out." We can see something as small as a speck of dust floating on the air. We can see stars far above us in the skies. We can detect the slightest movement. We can see the beauty or destruction of our environment. Like the Pharisees in the Gospel, "we see," but can we still be blind?

We can also see "in." So often many of us walk in the dark. We can be as blind as bats when it comes to the needs of our own hearts. Jesus offers an inward sight: the kind of sight that detects blindness within. It is the sight of Faith.

Jesus comes to bring us light for He is the light. He is the light of the world! He comes to give sight to our long-shuttered souls with the brilliance of God's own light. He comes to brighten our lives with a new vision of a shining future without and within.

We are invited by God to experience a response of faith. No one, not even Jesus, can order someone to have faith. Faith is a gift of the Father and is a free response to Jesus' invitation to come into the light of God's kingdom. We are required only to be open, like the blind man in this story, and be ready to receive what He offers us. Jesus has enlightened us, and has given us the "eyes" of faith. Faith-filled eyes "see." Faith-filled eyes recognize that there is more to life than meets the eye: winners do not always win; losers do not always lose; beggars can be rich; sinners can be justified; the sightless can see; and death can be the gateway to life.

Does the way you act in your daily life reveal your faith or deny it? Does the way you conduct yourself during your daily life enable others to "see" the light? This gift of faith gives us the opportunity to look inward to "see" if we are the light or darkness for others.

Take time to look deep inside yourself to see where you most need light. Allow yourself the time to look again at the world around you, to see God's grace in the ordinary things of life, and in the ordinary people you encounter.

As you progress through life, remember that Jesus has walked before you and shown you the way. He also walks with you to open your eyes so that you will not be blind, but "see."

Reflection:

"One thing I do know: I was blind, and now I see."

To better understand the above scriptural verse in context, you will find it helpful to read the entire passage: John 9:1–34.

Please reflect on the following:

1. In what way were the Pharisees blind, even though they could see?

   _____

   _____

2. What is spiritual blindness?

   _____

   _____

   Give examples:

   _____

   _____

3. What did Jesus mean when He said that the Pharisees were blind leaders of the blind?

   _____

   _____

4. Are you aware of your own blind spots?

   Can you make a list of them?

   _____

   _____

   Are you resolved to eradicate them?

   _____

   _____

5. Prayer:

   Create a pure heart in me, O God,
   And put a new spirit within me.
   Give me the joy of your salvation
   And make me willing to serve You.
   My sacrifice is a humble spirit.
   You will not spurn a contrite and humble heart.

   —Psalm 51

[7] Faith and Prejudice

"Jesus said to her in reply: O woman, great is your
faith! Let it be done for you as you wish."

—*The Gospel of Matthew*, chapter 15:27

The beautiful account of Jesus' interaction with the Canaanite
woman can be seen as an expression of God's love for everyone, without distinction (Matthew 15:21–27).

The Canaanite woman was different. She was a pagan and was
shunned by all Jews, including the apostles who wanted Jesus to get
rid of her. Jesus did not get rid of her. He accepted her and paid tribute
to her great faith which was rewarded with the healing of her daughter. How surprised and, perhaps, stunned the disciples must have been
to witness this miracle! Another one of their prejudices had gone up in
smoke.

Think for a moment of your five best friends. List them in your
mind. How many of them come from the same racial background as
you; have a similar type of education; make the same salary, and are
about your age? If you are like other people, you will find it easiest to
relate to people who are like you. It is very human to be more at home
with those who are like you, and who share your traditions and background.

Today's lesson is that people have to work hard at being Christian
for it means going outside your group and discovering that, differ-
ences aside, we are all one family. Today's Scripture is about God's
concern and love for all people. The Jews found this a bitter pill to
swallow. So, of course, do we. If you have any doubt about this, try

substituting Communist for Canaanite in today's Gospel story. Jesus does not look at appearances but at the individual whom he calls by name.

The truth of the matter is that God loves all his children: Capitalists and Communists, Protestants and Catholics, Buddhists and Hindus, Jews and Muslims. He wants us all to get along and we won't get along with each other if we keep raising barriers. If we put God's will, not man's will, at the center of our relationships we can learn to get along.

We are all family under God. Every time we try to get along with someone who is "different" we give credence to our belief that God is our Father, we are his children and Jesus is the way.

Reflection:

"Jesus said to her in reply: O woman, great is your faith! Let it be done for you as you wish."

To better understand the above scriptural verse in context, you will find it helpful to read the entire passage: Matthew 15:21–28.

Please reflect on the following:

1. How is the Canaanite woman similar to the Centurion in Matthew chapter 8?

    _____

    _____

    Were both of them pagans?

    _____

    _____

    Did both of these outsiders have the gift of faith?

    _____

    _____

2. This Gospel message invites you to step outside your comfort zone.

Can you accept those who are different from you as your brothers and sisters?

Think of those you have problems accepting.

Will you accept them, in your heart, as your brothers and sisters?

3. Jesus wants us to forgive others so we can be forgiven.

    Make a list of those you need to forgive:

    _____

    _____

    _____

    _____

    _____

4. Prayer:

> God grant me the grace to live one day at a time,
> To accept life's hardships as the way to peace.
> To take, as Jesus did, this sinful world
> As it is, not as I would have it.
> To trust that He will make all things right
> If I but surrender to His will,
> So that I may be content in this life
> And supremely happy in the next.

[8] Faith and Attitude

"'If only I can touch his cloak, I shall be cured.' Jesus turned around and saw her, and said, 'Courage, daughter! Your faith has saved you.'"

—*The Gospel of Matthew*, chapter 9:21–22

T
he woman who was suffering from hemorrhages for twelve years sneaked up behind Jesus to touch the tassel of his cloak because she believed that if she could just touch his cloak she would be cured. This incident tells us much about the quiet power of faith in the lives of those who trust in the Lord.

The woman's faith in today's Gospel was so strong and personal that she did not need to bother the Lord; she did not need to make demands on his time; nor did she see a need to disrupt what he was doing. All she needed to do was to demonstrate her personal faith in him, anonymously, by touching the tassel of his cloak. She thought nobody saw what she was doing, and indeed, Jesus' disciples saw nothing for when the Lord asked them, "Who touched me?" they denied any knowledge of the incident, and Peter answered "the people are all around you and crowding in on you" (Luke 8:45).

Jesus replied to his disciples, "Someone touched me, for I knew it when power went out of me" (Luke 8:46). The woman's silent anonymous faith connected with the Lord and the 'power' went out of him to cure her. This woman's faith was personal; it was unobtrusive; it was real. She had faith in the Lord, and her personal faith in him saved her.

Faith is a gift but it is a multifaceted gift.

There is faith as belief such as we recite in the profession of faith. But faith is more than the mere recitation of doctrines just as prayer is more than the mere recitation of words.

Faith is a matter of the heart; it is trust in the Lord who helps us and saves us in good times and in bad. It is an interior attitude like that of the woman in today's Gospel who had such trust in Jesus that, unknown to the disciples and all those crowding around the Lord, the power went out of Him to cure her.

Reflection:

"'If only I can touch his cloak, I shall be cured.' Jesus turned around and saw her, and said, 'Courage, daughter! Your faith has saved you.'"

To better understand the above scriptural verse in context, you will find it helpful to read the entire passage: Matthew 9:20–22.

Please reflect on the following:

1. What do the actions of the woman with the hemorrhage tell you about the quiet power of faith?

    _____

    _____

    Should faith be anonymous or should it be ostentatious?

    _____

    _____

    What about people who perform acts of faith to be seen like the Pharisees?

    _____

    _____

2. How is faith different from beliefs?

_____

_____

Give examples:

_____

_____

3. Do you respect others even if their beliefs differ to your own?

_____

_____

Are you prepared to engage in community activities with other denominations?

_____

_____

4. Prayer:

Grant, O Lord, that I may not be unduly anxious,
But, in everything, give thanks abundantly
By prayer and petition, made known to You,
So that your peace, which surpasses all understanding,
May guard my heart and my thoughts.
In Jesus' name, Amen.

[9] Faith and Trials

"He said to them, why are you so terrified, O you of little faith?"

—*The Gospel of Matthew*, chapter 8:26

P eople often tell you after experiencing a great trial: "If it wasn't for my faith, I would never have got through this." Faith can be a great comfort in times of trouble; it can give you the power and the strength to persevere, to hold on, to wait it out (whatever it may be) and to survive the test.

There are two great gifts in life: the gift of health and the gift of faith. What health is to the body, faith is to the soul. The Gospel is full of stories about faith: the faith of Bartimaeus who had his sight restored; the faith of the Centurion whose servant was cured; and St. Thomas' shout of faith: "My Lord and My God" when he experienced the risen Lord.

In this Scripture, the disciples are terrified because the boat they are in is "being swamped by waves." The seas inspired an awesome fear in ancient times because mariners did not have strong boats or sophisticated instruments like we have today. While the disciples are terrified, Jesus is quietly asleep. Notice the contrast!

The great Dutch painter, Rembrandt, depicts this scene in one of his greatest paintings. The faces of the disciples are disfigured with terror as the waves threaten to topple the boat while the Lord is sleeping quietly with his head upon a cushion. This painting shows the stark contrast between terror and faith; the terror of the disciples and the calm faith of the Lord.

At times, we feel overwhelmed by life and its problems. Only a calm faith can hold us up in times like this when everything seems to be coming unglued. People ask me today: "Have you ever seen so many bad things happening at the same time? What is the meaning of this? Is it the end of the world?" A recent poll indicates that 41 percent of Americans think the end of the world is upon us.

The Lord cautions us not to be misled by stories about the end of the world if these stories should distract us from following Him and listening to His word. He states: "of that day and hour no one knows, neither the angels of heaven, nor the Son, but the Father alone" (Matthew 24:36). If the Son of God did not worry about the end of the world, why should we? We have a more important task at hand: to live our lives calmly with faith in God. If you have faith in God and seek his kingdom, everything else will fall into place.

Faith is a wonderful gift. It is a gift that helps us remain calm in times of personal trial and natural calamities.

Reflection:

"He said to them, why are you so terrified, O you of little faith?"

To better understand the above scriptural verse in context, you will find it helpful to read the entire passage: Matthew 8:23–27.
Please reflect on the following:

1. Our age is an anxious age!

    How does faith cure anxiety or fear?

    _____

    _____

    Give examples from your own life.

    _____

    _____

2. Why is faith to the soul what health is to the body?

    _____

    _____

    Give examples of the beneficial effects of faith on your soul.

    _____

    _____

3.   Why are people preoccupied with the end of the world?

_____

_____

What does Jesus say about the end of the world?

_____

_____

Show how a living faith is the answer to preoccupations over the end of the world.

_____

_____

4.   Prayer:

> Trust in the Lord completely
> More than in yourself.
> In everything you do,
> Put God first, and last.
> He is the Alpha and the Omega,
> The beginning and the end.
> He will protect you,
> He will crown your efforts with success.

[10] Faith and Obstacles

"I assure you that whoever tells this mountain to get up and throw itself into the sea... it will be done for him."

—The Gospel of Mark, chapter 11:23

There's a story about an old woman in Donegal (Ireland), where the land is mountainy. She prayed all night that God would remove the mountain in front of her house because it prevented her from keeping a watchful eye on the sheep that tended to wander away over the mountain out of sight. She got out of bed in the morning after a feverish night of praying; opened the door of the house; and looked out aghast: "I knew it would still be there," she said, shaking her head in disbelief.

Jesus says in this Gospel that if we have enough faith we could move mountains. What does He mean by this? What kind of mountains is he referring to? Is he talking about the mountains of Donegal for which the landscape is justifiably famous? No! He is telling us that with faith in Him, we can overcome anything? Could it be, that the reason we are not seeing miracles in our lives, is because we are focusing on the wrong things, instead of God? We keep thinking that we have to do this and do that in order to have enough faith to receive the miracle we want. What we do not realize, is that God never asks us to muster up any faith by ourselves. You see, faith is a gift from God; it is not something we create ourselves; it rewards us when we trust in the giver of this gift.

So then, how do we have the faith that moves problems as big as mountains?

We exercise this kind of faith when we allow Jesus to minister to us. Instead of focusing on ourselves we need to trust in the Lord. When people settle for their own faith, more often than not, nothing happens. But when they trust in the Lord, wonders happen, sometimes without them even knowing it.

When Peter walked on water, he did so not through his own faith, but through his faith in the Lord. When he was focused on Jesus, he walked on the turbulent waters despite the huge waves. However, the moment he stopped trusting in the Lord and focused on the 'terrifying' waves instead, he immediately sank. Were the waves any larger or more dangerous than those during the brief moment when he walked on water? Of course not! The only difference is that when he stopped trusting in the Lord, he allowed his surroundings to overwhelm him and engulf him.

Always remember, God is the giver of faith. He always has the first and last word in every situation. Through faith in Him, we allow Him to work in our lives.

By trusting in Him, we are in effect asking Him to work on our behalf to bring about the highest good in our lives. Instead of constantly worrying and fretting about what we can do to solve our problems, we can leave it to the Lord. We need to stop running away from Him, and run towards Him and allow Him to help us with our problems.

So then, whenever you are in trouble, simply look away from your circumstances, and trust in the Lord. There is absolutely no way you can trust in Him without your situation improving.

This is the faith that moves mountains.

Reflection:

"I assure you that whoever tells this mountain to get up and throw itself into the sea... it will be done for him."

To better understand the above scriptural verse in context, you will find it helpful to read the entire passage: Mark 11:20–26.

Please reflect on the following:

1. How does faith as trust in the Lord reward us?

    _____

    _____

    Give examples from Scripture.

    _____

    _____

    Give examples from your own life.

    _____

    _____

2. Why did Peter's faith falter when he walked on water?

    _____

    _____

3. Is faith trust in your own powers or in the Lord's power?

_____

_____

4. Prayer:

> The mountains may move ,
> The hills may disappear,
> But my kindness
> Shall never leave you,
> Says the Lord.
> My promise of peace for you
> Shall never be broken.

[11] Faith and Blindness

"I came into this world for judgment, so that those who do not see might see, and those who do see might become blind."

—*The Gospel of John*, chapter 9:39

T he story of the cure of the man born blind (John 9:1–41) is also a story about the judgment of Jesus; for He came into this world so that those who do not see might see, and, conversely, so that those who presume to see might become blind. A blind beggar draws Jesus' attention. Jesus gives him elaborate directions, which the blind man follows, and he comes back seeing. All he knows is that once he could not see and now he sees.

His neighbors take him to the Pharisees. This was standard operating procedure at that time... so far, so good. But then things turn sour. The now-seeing, blind man becomes a stumbling block for the religious leaders. The educated and religiously sophisticated Pharisees cross-examine the poor fellow. Rather than rejoicing in his newfound vision, they castigate him for violating the Sabbath since he was cured by Jesus on the Sabbath. The Pharisees cannot see beyond their fanatical obsession with the details of the law. That is their blindness. They could see with their eyes, but they were spiritually blind.

There is a lot of back-and-forth in this story, and in the end, the blind man stands alone. His parents are cowed and bullied by the Pharisees who are like blind teachers teaching the blind (Matthew 15:12–14).

In their confusion, the parents do not speak up for their son. Their fear has blinded them. The establishment condemns him. The man born blind is thrown out of the temple, that vital center of Jewish life.

Then Jesus comes to him. Of course He does. He asks simple and direct questions of the man, and the man answers simply and directly. In the end, the light of faith is added to physical sight as the man who was once blind sees: When asked by Jesus: "Do you believe in the son of man?" he answered: "I do believe, Lord."

Many people go through life with eyes, but they see not. They are spiritually blind. Often, they are blinded by their own greed, arrogance, attachment to possessions or by hypocrisy like the Pharisees. What is your blind spot? What do you have to pluck out of your life, so that you can see? Are you blind to the needs of others? Are you blind to the prejudices within you? Are you blind to the good news of the Gospel?

Jesus says in St. John's Gospel (John 9:39): "I came into this world for judgment, so that those who do not see might see." Ask the Lord to heal you of spiritual blindness. Ask the Lord to bless you with His gift of spiritual sight to understand His word and to put it into practice.

Reflection:

"I came into this world for judgment, so that those who do not see might see, and those who do see might become blind."

To better understand the above scriptural verse in context, you will find it helpful to read the entire passage: John 9:1–14.

Please reflect on the following:

1. What was the cause of the Pharisees' spiritual blindness?

   _____

   _____

2. What are the signs of spiritual blindness?

   Give examples:

   _____

   _____

3. Give some examples of the worst forms of spiritual blindness in today's society:

   _____

   _____

4. Prayer:

> The just person does not fear bad news,
> Nor live in dread of what may happen.
> He is confident that God will rescue him
> And save him out of all his troubles.
> He will walk calmly, never fearing
> The evil of the world or human wickedness.

[12] Faith and Gratitude

"Has none but this foreigner returned to give thanks to God? Then he said to him: stand up and go; your faith has saved you."

—*The Gospel of Luke*, chapter 17:19

This Gospel passage throws the spotlight on an essential dimension of faith; namely, gratitude. The Gospel tells the story about Jesus healing the ten lepers and how only one returned to give thanks. Gratitude is an expression of faith. Wherever there was no gratitude or belief in Him, Jesus became distressed and, on occasion, He could not perform any miracles (Matthew 13:58). Addressing the Samaritan who showed gratitude, Jesus said: "Your faith has saved you."

There is no such thing as an empty gift. Faith is the greatest gift of all; it sets people free; it offers healing and release from the chains of a sinful life; it gives light to the mind, power to the soul. Faith cannot exist without the response of gratitude because it is such a wonderful, life-giving gift as the example of the Samaritan leper, who returned to give thanks to Jesus, demonstrates.

The Samaritan in this Gospel story knew how to be grateful, and his gratitude, after receiving Christ's healing power, found expression in a burst of praise.

The gratitude required of faith implies three things: The giver (God), the receiver (you), and the community (the Church). For the Samaritan it was not sufficient to slip away quietly, after he was healed, like the other nine. He was a grateful man, and he expressed his thanks to Jesus for the gift he received in the presence of the community. His gratitude could not be contained or kept to himself; he had to express it publicly, loud and clear.

The Samaritan's gratitude can quite properly be called Eucharistic (meaning, Thanksgiving). He returned thanks to Jesus in the presence of the people. Whenever you receive communion during mass, think about that. No need to be glum or tight lipped. Be grateful that you can receive Christ with the worshiping community; be grateful and show it in the way you live. You cannot receive Christ, worthily, in communion if you do not see Christ in your neighbors, your brothers and sisters, just as you cannot love God whom you do not see if you do not love your neighbor whom you do see.

There is so much we need to be grateful for in our lives. Be grateful for the gift of faith which comes to us from above. Be grateful for the support and love of family, friends, and fellow travelers. Be not only grateful; be ready to show it like the Samaritan leper in today's Gospel story.

Reflection:

"Has none but this foreigner returned to give thanks to God? Then he said to him: stand up and go; your faith has saved you."

To better understand the above scriptural verse in context, you will find it helpful to read the entire passage: Luke 17:11–19.

Please reflect on the following:

1. How does the Samaritan leper's faith contrast with the other nine?

   Give examples:

   _____

   _____

2. Wherever gratitude was absent, Jesus could perform no miracles (Matthew 13:58).

   Does your faith possess the spirit of gratitude?

   _____

   _____

3. List some of the blessings of faith for which you are grateful.

   _____

   _____

4.   The gratitude required of faith requires three things.

What are they?

_____

_____

_____

5.   Prayer:

Put your trust in God alone.
If God is with you
Who can be against you?
God did not spare His Son
But gave Him up for you.
Will he not surely give you
Everything else besides?

[13] Faith and Life

"Whoever loves his life loses it and whoever hates his life in this world will preserve it for life eternal."

—The Gospel of John, chapter 12:25

Everyone wants to cling to life; to seek any remedy that will make life easier and prolong it. There is nothing wrong with that! So why then does Jesus say: "Whoever loves his life loses it and whoever hates his life in this world will preserve it for life eternal?"

The answer is that there are different types of life. The world offers one way of life while faith offers another. Jesus did not come to condemn the world, He came to save it. The world that is compromised by sin— greed, rapaciousness, war, torture, hatred, and enmity of all sorts—is a world that promotes not true life but death. That is why Jesus says: "Whoever hates his life in this world will preserve it for life eternal." He wants us to possess true life by rejecting the false way of life which the world offers.

There are many people who embrace the false way of life the world offers. They give themselves over to lives of greed and ruthless competition. They accumulate large fortunes of money at the expense of God's environment, God's children, and God's word; and they get away with it for they are protected by the principalities and powers of this world (which they helped create).

The Christian, on the other hand, is called to live the good life of the Gospel in the world while not being of it (John 17:15–16). The Christian gets into trouble when he/she dilutes the life of the Gospel with the life of the world. The Gospel is meant to be a leaven in the world. It is meant to purify the world; to save the world from itself; to renew it and redeem it. There are many wonderful things in our world, however, which enhance and improve the human condition. Advances in science, medicine, technology, and education, for example, have improved the quality of human life for so many people. The Gospel does not seek to reject these worthwhile improvements in human living; it builds on them to create a better world that is free from the corrosion of greed, self-interest, inequality, hubris, vengeance, and hate. In this way, the Gospel is described as a leaven in the world because it brings to fullness the possibilities of man in the world.

The way to guard ourselves against mixing the life of the Gospel with the "life" of the world is to be familiar with the scriptures. By familiar, I mean: living according to the scriptures, not just reading or listening to them in Church. Before the scriptures were ever written, there were people who lived them. The early Christians were called "people of the way." Jesus lived what we read about in the New Testament, but He did not leave us anything in writing. It was His disciples who wrote down what He did and what He said, for our benefit. If Christians are genuinely familiar with the scriptures, they will be protected from the world, and the world with all its false values will not overpower them.

They will have a fuller and better life, here and now, and inherit eternal happiness in the next life.

Reflection:

"Whoever loves his life loses it and whoever hates his life in this world will preserve it for life eternal."

To better understand the above scriptural verse in context, you will find it helpful to read the entire passage: John 12:20–26.

Please reflect on the following:

1. How does a faith perspective on life contrast with a worldly way of life?

   Give examples:

   _____

   _____

2. What does Jesus mean by, "Whoever loves his life loses it?"

   _____

   _____

   Give examples from your own experience:

   _____

   _____

3. Can you mix the Gospel with the selfishness of the world?

    _____

    _____

    Give examples of this false dilution of values.

    _____

    _____

    What about your own life? Do you follow the false values of the world?

4. Prayer:

    Be content in everything
    Whether it be in want or in plenty.
    You can do everything the Lord asks
    Through the grace of Jesus Christ
    Whose power is perfected when you are weak.

[14] Faith and Mercy

"Jesus, son of David, have mercy on me."

—*The Gospel of Mark*, chapter 10:47

In this scripture, the blind beggar, Bartimaeus, comes across as a vulnerable seeker . Everybody in the neighborhood, it seems, knew this blind son of Timaeus. People advised him to quiet down, not to be upsetting himself and others who were quietly going about their business. All the while, Bartimaeus ignored their admonitions and boldly called out, *"Jesus, son of David, have mercy on me!"* Eventually, the same people who were fed up with Bartimaeus helped him on his way to Jesus. Sometimes it works like that. We are helped and led to the Lord by people we would never expect to help us. The Lord's mercy manifests itself in strange ways.

When Jesus called Bartimaeus to come forward, the blind beggar asked for the obvious: that he might see. His faith was able to draw forth the miracle of sight and his eyes fell on the One who brought him wholeness of body and spirit. Then, Jesus told him: "Be on your way! Your faith has healed you" (Mark 10:52).

Bartimaeus chose to follow the way of Jesus. This following of Jesus "on the way" refers to much more than Bartimaeus' new–found ability to walk better, now that he could see. It focuses on a new Bartimaeus entirely, one who has become transformed through the mercy of Christ. This is a following of a different kind; this is a more challenging walk for Bartimaeus. From then on this new-sighted man became a faithful man. Bartimaeus not only got his eyesight back; he gained the kind of foresight, hindsight and insight that conforms to that of the merciful Christ who called him forth from his original blindness.

The journey of Jesus led to Jerusalem (The place of His full and final self-giving) and to the glory of the Resurrection. Bartimaeus—vulnerable, stumbling and seeking, had to learn this as he went along. So do we; we are also asked to take in the whole journey. How do we set out? We set out with the assurance of faith in God's mercy which tells us that this journey is not our own. We will know we are on the right way if and when our lives are conformed to that of Christ who called us forth out of the dark valley into the highway to heaven.

In contrast to the rich young man, who belonged to a higher social status than Bartimaeus, and rejected the invitation of the Lord to follow Him (Mark 10:22), Bartimaeus encountered Jesus "on the way," and followed Him. There is an important lesson here. You don't have to be important or distinguished to follow Jesus; and Bartimaeus makes it clear that those at the bottom of the social order are just as favored in the eyes of God, as those at the top! Bartimaeus is a clear case of the healing power of God's mercy "perfected in weakness." Thus Bartimaeus stands out as a symbol of God's mercy for all of us.

Reflection:

"Jesus, son of David, have mercy on me."

To better understand the above scriptural verse in context, you will find it helpful to read the entire passage: Mark 10:46–52.

Please reflect on the following:

1. Bartimaeus shows that the least among us is as favored, before God, as the highest among us.

    How does this affect your attitude towards others?

    Give examples:

    _____

    _____

2. Have you been helped in your faith journey by people you never expected to help you?

    Give examples:

    _____

    _____

3. How does the assurance of faith in God's mercy show us the way, and protect us on our Christian journey?

Give examples:

_____

_____

4. Prayer:

> Cast your cares upon the Lord,
> He is always thinking about you.
> He watches over you day and night
> That you might not trip or fall.
> He has taken all our cares.
> Let us trust in His mercy completely.

[15] Faith and Example

"Your light must shine before others so they will see the good things you do and praise your Heavenly Father."

—*The Gospel of Matthew*, chapter 5:16

There was a man who used to gamble and drink a lot before he converted to Christ. His fellow workers were fond of teasing him: "Surely a man like you doesn't believe in miracles and all that bible stuff. How could you believe that Jesus turned water into wine?" The man's reply was: "Whether He turned water into wine or not, I do not know, but in my home I have seen Him turn my love of beer into love of family." The strongest argument in defense of the Christian faith is to be found not in words, but in example; by showing the practical difference faith can make in your life. No one can argue against the proof of a changed life!

In today's scripture passage, the Lord asks us to let the light of our faith shine in our lives by the things we do. This is the faith that transforms a person's life into something positive and productive.

Have you ever tried to share your faith with others? How did you go about it? Did you to try to convince others that your beliefs were better than theirs? This kind of approach to faith is called polemical. A polemical approach may sometimes be necessary in defending the faith against those who attack it with intellectual arguments. It can reassure the believer but it seldom converts the unbeliever.

A more effective way of presenting the faith is to show the blessings that faith has brought about in your life. This is called testimony or bearing witness to the faith. This is what Jesus is talking about in today's scripture when He says we should let our light shine before others so they will see the good things you do and praise your Heavenly Father (Matthew 5:16).

We can learn from St. Paul who tried to win the Athenians over to the Christian faith with erudite, philosophical arguments (Acts 17). These sophisticated and logical explanations of the faith didn't impress his learned audience who loved debates for the sake of debates. They only made fun of Paul and responded: "We will hear you another day about this" (Acts 17:32).

St. Paul had a change of heart after this when it came to preaching the good news.

When he arrived in Corinth later he did not speak with "lofty words or wisdom" (1 Corinthians 2:1) as he had done in Athens. He spoke plainly, and told the story of Jesus Christ who was crucified for our sins. The people of Corinth came to believe in Jesus, not because of St. Paul's eloquence, but on the power of the living God acting in their lives (1 Corinthians 2:5).

Let us strive to spread the good news of the Lord's kingdom by the power of faith "acting in our lives."

Reflection:

"Your light must shine before others so they will see the good things you do and praise your Heavenly Father."

To better understand the above scriptural verse in context, you will find it helpful to read the entire passage: Matthew 5:13–16.
Please reflect on the following:

1. How do you let the light of faith shine through in your life?

    Give examples:

    _____

    _____

2. Why is faith described as the light?

    How does the light of faith dispel the darkness from your life?

    Give examples.

    _____

    _____

3. What is the best argument in defense of the faith?

    _____

    _____

Would you prefer witness over polemics?

Give reasons for your preference.

_____

_____

4. Prayer:

> Lord, let Your light shine
> Within and about me.
> Have no worry about anything
> But pray about everything.
> Tell the Lord your needs,
> Giving thanks for His blessings.
> His peace, more wonderful
> Than the mind can conceive.
> The Lord's peace will keep your
> Thoughts and your hearts quiet
> And at rest as you trust in Him.

[16] Faith and Money

"No one can serve two masters. Either you will hate the
one and love the other or you will be devoted to the one
and despise the other. You cannot serve God and
Mammon."

—*The Gospel of Matthew*, chapter 6:24

The word, mammon, is an Aramaic word that refers to wealth
and property. Jesus is asking us in this scripture to make a
choice between God and riches. Surviving in our world demands that we make choices. The disciples of Jesus had to choose between Him and the gods of society. Which will it be? Jesus or the world?

Choices are the tools we use to chisel our personalities from the hard stone of life. Let us ponder the choices we make in life, especially the most fundamental of all our choices: who will be our God? We sometimes imagine that modern-day people rarely, if ever, worship false gods. Well, it all depends on what is meant by false gods.

Do you accept the god of our society with all the materialistic values and self-centered pursuits this social god offers you? Or, will you turn aside from the spirit of materialism and walk instead with Jesus, the God who loves the poor and the downtrodden, the homeless and the hungry, the deprived and the forgotten? What will be your choice? Will you invest your life in becoming secure and comfortable, rich and powerful, or will you use your gift of faith to bring justice to the poor, care to the forgotten and love to the unlovable? Either you stand in faith with Jesus and walk in His way or you walk with the idols of the marketplace toward power and worldly prestige. You cannot have it both ways. You must make a choice. That is what faith in Christ is all about.

Oscar Romero was the archbishop of San Salvador, a conservative man who began his ministry by leading his archdiocese along traditional paths. He was a good man, a man well loved by all decent people. He started to build a new cathedral and strengthen his diocesan seminary. Then, he was confronted by the oppression and the poverty of his people. He canceled his building plans, moved refugees into the seminary grounds and began to speak out against the tyranny he saw everywhere around him. He made a choice, a faith decision that opted for the poor and the oppressed. After several threats, a group of assassins murdered him while he was saying Mass in a local hospital.

Many would-be followers abandoned Jesus after his challenging words about the lure of riches; the Eucharist; and the ways of the world. They would have wished that Jesus had not challenged them the way he did. They must have longed for the days when they could have followed Him without having to make such hard choices. Yet, they did have to choose. His true followers had to make a faith decision to follow Him. They could not avoid that choice nor can we.

We may imagine we can accept Christ and the ways of our world but we deceive ourselves. Faith involves a choice: "You cannot serve God and mammon" (Matthew 6:24).

Reflection:

"No one can serve two masters. Either you will hate the one and love the other or you will be devoted to the one and despise the other."

To better understand the above scriptural verse in context, you will find it helpful to read the entire passage: Matthew 6:19–24.

Please reflect on the following:

1. Everyone makes choices.
    Why is it important to choose God over money?

    _____

    _____

2. Why did Archbishop Romero abandon his original choice to build a new Cathedral?

    _____

    _____

3. How has your faith decision to follow Jesus influenced your life?

    Give examples:

    _____

    _____

4. What sacrifices are you making now to serve God instead of money?

   Give examples:

   _____

   _____

5. Prayer:

   Bless the Lord, oh my soul.
   All my being bless His holy name.
   He pardons all your iniquities.
   He heals all your ills.
   He redeems your life from destruction,
   He crowns you with kindness and compassion.

   —Psalm 103

[17] Faith and Openness

"And He could do no miracles there, except that He placed His hands on a few sick people and healed them."

—*The Gospel of Mark*, chapter 6:5

An old man was wondering if his wife had a hearing problem. So one night, while his wife was sitting in her lounge chair, he sneaked behind her and said softly: "Honey, can you hear me?" He got no response. He moved a little closer and said again, "Honey, can you hear me?" Still, he got no response. Finally, he moved right next her and said, "Honey, can you hear me?" This time she looked up with surprise in her eyes and replied, "For the third time, Henry, Yes, I can hear you!" Now, who had the hearing problem? The man or his wife?

We are all too ready to blame others for a breakdown in communication when we ourselves might be responsible for the lack of communication. In today's Gospel we read of a serious breakdown in communication between Jesus and his townspeople. It was so serious that Jesus was unable to perform any miracles there because of the people's lack of faith.

This was a scandalous situation that Jesus, in His hometown, among His own kinfolk, could not perform any miracles. Not that he would not but that he simply could not. It was impossible for Jesus to perform miracles in this situation where there was no faith. Jesus, as the Son of God, can do all things for his people, but He needs our openness to the gift of faith to release His power. Remember the wonderful story in the Gospel about the woman with the flow of blood. Many people were touching and pushing against Jesus, but nothing happened because they did not touch Him with faith. But as soon as the woman of faith touched Him, healing power came out of Him. We have the capacity to disable Jesus by our closed attitude or lack of openness. Like a switch that turns a light on, an open heart is the switch that turns God on whereas hardness of heart is the switch that turns God off.

Jesus' kinsfolk took offence at Him for his inability to perform miracles among them. Do you sometimes wonder at God's apparent inactivity in a world of corruption and injustice? When people are tempted to blame God for doing nothing, is it not possible that God can do nothing because of people's hardness of heart?

Why did Jesus' own kinsfolk not have faith in Him? Jesus says it is because "Prophets are not without honor, except in their hometown, and among their own kin, and in their own house" (Mark 6:4). The kinsfolk of Jesus thought they knew everything there was to know about Him, and they were not impressed. People who are converts to the faith often do better than old timers in the faith because there is a tendency among old timers to think that they know everything there is to know about the faith. This becomes an obstacle to experiencing the mercy and power of God, which is offered anew each day through the same old Gospel, and the same old sacraments, and the good example of the same old people. This Gospel is a warning against the kind of smugness that smothers or crushes the workings of the Holy Spirit in our midst; the kind of smugness that kills faith.

This Gospel tells the story of people who met Jesus, but left without a blessing. As we meet Jesus in His word, in His sacraments, and in those around us, let us resolve to be open to His gift and not to leave without a blessing.

Reflection:

"And He could do no miracles there, except that He placed His hands on a few sick people and healed them."

To better understand the above scriptural verse in context, you will find it helpful to read the entire passage: Mark 6:1–6.

Please reflect on the following:

1. Why could Jesus not perform any miracles among His own kinsfolk and in His own hometown?

   _____

   _____

2. How did lack of openness manifest itself among Jesus' kinsfolk?

   Give examples.

   _____

   _____

3. Contrast the faith of the woman who touched Jesus's garment with the lack of faith of His kinsfolk.

   _____

   _____

4. How does lack of faith manifest itself among people today?

   Give examples:

   _____

   _____

5. Prayer:

> Oh God, who through the folly of the Cross
> Has taught us the surpassing knowledge
> Of our divine savior, Jesus Christ.
> Grant that I may reject temptation
> And the errors of the world
> To become steadfast and loyal in the Faith.

[18] Faith and End Times

"When you hear of wars and insurrections, do not be terrified; for such things must happen first, but it will not immediately be the end."

—*The Gospel of Luke*, chapter 21:9

Year in, year out, somebody takes on the task of naively reading the signs of the end-times for us. We have heard the prophets of doom, of Armageddon, of the end of the world who have predicted the destruction of our planet. But, our world still keeps turning and we keep churning along.

Chapter twenty-one of the Gospel of Luke offers an important insight about the end of the world. We do not know when it will be. We can expect apocalyptic events such as 9/11 and disastrous hurricanes like Katrina in New Orleans. But these events do not mean that the end is in sight. We can expect to be set to by earth-shattering changes in our society. It comes with the territory. The fragmentation of the world around us calls for steadfast patience and faith, not panic. No need to draw our wagons in a circle and let the world fall apart. This reaction won't wash. It is not based on scripture and it won't help bring about God's reign.

As Christians, we rest our case on our faith that the risen Lord is with us, active and effective. So we must open our hearts and minds to the great work at hand, and "not be terrified."

Sometimes we are inclined to think about the good old days. Our selective memory inclines to convince us that they existed. The Gospel focuses on the good new days when Jesus' message will be alive and well, here and now, in our daily lives.

Be attentive to the signs of the times and try to make your community, your world, a better place to live in with God's help. Do not be preoccupied about the end of the world which is beyond your understanding. Focus on the present and how you can make it better. That is all you can do.

Savor the grace of the present moment; try to enjoy it for what it is rather than for what it is not. You are given eighty six thousand, four hundred moments every day. Over twenty-eight thousand of those moments, more or less, are given over to sleep. So, make the best of the remaining fifty eight thousand moments of your day. They are more valuable to you and to the Lord than the same number in dollars. They are the inestimable gifts of life itself which can never be replicable once they are gone. So, reach out to the person beside you; share with him or her the grace of a smile; a word of encouragement or gratitude; a blessing or a timely word of healing. Do not be anxious about tomorrow.

Tomorrow can take care of itself. Each day has enough problems of its own (Matthew 6:34).

Reflection:

"When you hear of wars and insurrections, do not be terrified; for such things must happen first, but it will not immediately be the end."

To better understand the above scriptural verse in context, you will find it helpful to read the entire passage: Luke 21:7–11.

Please reflect on the following:

1. How should you prepare for the end days, and what should be your focus?

    Give examples:

    _____

    _____

2. How can you be attentive to the grace of the present moment?

    Give examples:

    _____

    _____

3. What can you do to witness to the risen Lord in your life?

    Give examples:

    _____

    _____

4. Prayer:

> Oh God, whose Providence never fails
> To direct our lives according to the proper design,
> Protect us from all that might harm us.
> Grant us Your grace so that everything
> We do might work for our good.

[19] Faith and Sacrifice

"If your right eye causes you to sin, tear it out and throw it away. It is better for you to lose one of your members than to have your whole body thrown into Gehenna."

—*The Gospel of Matthew*, chapter 5:29–30

Why would the Lord recommend that we mutilate our bodies which we should respect as precious gifts of God? Are not our bodies temples of the Holy Spirit (1 Corinthians 6:19–20). Why does He tell us in chapter five of St. Matthew's Gospel to tear out your right eye, if it causes you to sin, and throw it away?

It is obvious that Jesus is asking us to make the sacrifice of plucking out, not our right eye, but that part of our psychological being that is preventing us from entering into his kingdom. He wants us to free ourselves from spiritual blindness that keeps us in the dark; that prevents us from seeing with the light of faith.

The eye is the lamp of the body, but if it is in darkness, it will not let the light in. All knowledge, according to Aristotle, comes through the senses. The sense of sight is a wonderful gift, but it must be used creatively and wisely. There is sight and there is sight; there is physical sight and there is spiritual sight. The lusting eye that excites depraved cravings within the heart; the ugly mind that reaches out for what it does not own; must be cut off or sacrificed if we are to see with the light of faith.

People in Jesus' day did not appreciate the wonders He was doing. He said: "They have eyes but they see not." Many today go through life like blind people or with blinkers on; they see what they want to see and they don't see or open themselves up to what they should see. They see the bad in others and they refuse to see that their blindness or harsh judgment derive from their bad attitudes. They will not know the truth unless they pluck out the spiritual blindness from within that prevents them from seeing themselves and others as they truly are. Then, will their eyes be open; then will they see with the light of faith. It is so easy when you are spiritually blind to "see the speck in your brother's eye, and ignore the boulder in your own eye" (Matthew 7:3).

The Lord has given us the gift of sight to be used for our benefit; to observe and understand the works of His creation; even to read His word in the scriptures. This is a wonderful gift, this gift of physical sight, but it must be accompanied by a sense of sacrifice if we want to see beyond our sensory experience. Meditation on the Scripture; openness to the Holy Spirit, the spirit of truth; will help us to penetrate beyond the surface of things and enter into the spiritual world of awareness, meaning, and love.

This sense of sacrifice or self-denial is an awesome, personal attribute. Cultivate it in your life, and use it well.

Reflection:

"If your right eye causes you to sin, tear it out and throw it away. It is better for you to lose one of your members than to have your whole body thrown into Gehenna."

To better understand the above scriptural verse in context, you will find it helpful to read the entire passage: Matthew 5:21–48.

Please reflect on the following:

1. Does the Lord recommend in this scripture that we mutilate our bodies?

   What type of sacrifice does He recommend?

   Give examples:

   _____

   _____

2. Make a list of some of the things you need to sacrifice or eradicate from your life if you are to see with the light of faith.

   _____

   _____

3. Contrast physical sight with the spiritual sight of faith.

   _____

   _____

4. Prayer:

> Trusting in Your compassion Lord,
> We approach You eagerly
> Through the purifying action of Your grace,
> So as to be cleansed of our sins
> And walk blamelessly in Your sight.

[20] Faith and Peace

"The fruit of righteousness is sown in peace for those who cultivate peace."

—The Letter of James, chapter 3:18

Were you ever a member of a gang when you were a child? Do you remember how being a member of that gang meant that you were loyal to the group and to its code of behavior? It seems childish now but there is a lesson here. Something similar happens to us when we take the Gospel seriously. We become members of a special group. What used to give us a feeling of success and well-being in the old gang no longer has an attraction for us. Is there any wonder that we should be treated differently by those who still cling to the old gang? We may be a threat to our old companions, a contradiction to their way of life. We now are different and let us face it: we have moved beyond the values and beliefs of the old gang. This is a good time to reflect on what it means to belong to this new group which cultivates, peacefully, "the fruit of righteousness".

Fr. Jim Carney was an American Jesuit who worked in Central America. More than most, he took the Gospel seriously; he cultivated peace, and the fruit of righteousness among the poor and he paid the price. Few understood him. Many religious men and women shied away from him for he identified radically with the poor Indian peasants of Honduras. He lived in a shack like theirs, ate their food, shared their frustrations and championed their struggles for freedom. The government saw him as a threat when he asked that the poor be treated righteously and be allowed to own the land they worked. His rejection was complete only when he was taken into custody by the army, tortured and killed. Like Jesus before him, he experienced the ultimate rejection for doing God's will.

Human beings are social animals. Like the monkey or the coyote or the wolf, we run with the pack. We need to belong. But, we need to belong to something greater than ourselves if we are to avoid loneliness and meaninglessness. Many drug addicts begin their addiction by trying to be a part of a group. That is bad, of course, but understandable. Today, many people try to escape loneliness by belonging to a virtual world of the Internet and social media. But, the more they immerse themselves in this new virtual world, the lonelier they become because they cut themselves off from the real world of human contact.

A Christian is a person of peace who is called to wage peace not war. For a time, after your awakening to the Gospel, you may feel rejected by the groups to which you once were a part. This is very painful, but it is a part of the conversion process which leads to finding new friends who share your new values of working, peacefully, for a better environment—a better world.

A disciple in Jesus' day was a person who gave up everything to follow the master. He lived with the master, listened to his every word, and shaped his life to make it like the master's life. It meant total dedication, a relationship more intense than a marriage.

We are called to be disciples of Jesus. When we heed that call, we cut off many dysfunctional relationships in order to deepen our relationship with Christ and with His people. We have to break the old cycle of dependency in order to spread the "fruit of righteousness which is sown in peace for those who cultivate peace" (James 3:18).

Reflection:

"The fruit of righteousness is sown in peace for those who cultivate peace."

To better understand the above scriptural verse in context, you will find it helpful to read the entire passage: James 3:13–18

Please reflect on the following:

1. Why is it important to belong to a faith community that shares the same values?

    Give examples:

    _____

    _____

2. There will always be martyrs for the faith like Fr. Carney in Honduras.

    Give examples of some modern-day martyrs who have waged peace not war:

    _____

    _____

3. What is a disciple?

    _____

4. Why is Jesus referred to as Master?

_____

_____

5. Prayer:

> Look with favor, Lord, on my prayer.
> Whatever I ask for in prayer
> You will grant it in Your goodness.
> You know my thoughts
> And the secrets of my heart.
> Make me a vessel of Your Divine Will.

[21] Faith and Compassion

"He pitied them, for they were like sheep without a shepherd; and He began to teach them at great length."

—*The Gospel of Mark*, chapter 6:34

You wake up to a hot summer morning outside. It is Sunday. Inside the house, the air conditioner is purring contentedly. Gradually, you begin to think of getting up and going to church. You dread the thought of the heat, the smell of the pews in church, the closeness of all those restless bodies and, perhaps, the long sermon. "Maybe I should just stay here," you think. "I can worship God without being packed like sardines in a pew. After all, whether I go to church or not I can worship God in my own way, in spirit and in my own bed."

But, can you? Without the gathering, how can you call yourself part of the gathered, the church?

In today's scripture passage we are compared to sheep and Jesus is the Good Shepherd. He has gathered us into the fold. He has done this the hard way-by shedding his blood and giving His life for us. Through Jesus the shepherd, we now may enjoy real and lasting life, the life of a people united in love to one another and to God.

The Gospel of Mark, chapter six, offers a brief, but touching account of how the Good Shepherd acts. Jesus' apostles had just returned from their journey. They had much to tell him, much to ask. Surely Jesus had much to say. So Jesus has compassion for his apostles and takes them away to be alone with them. But there is no rest for Jesus. The crowd follows Him. Upon seeing the people, Jesus cannot suppress his shepherding instincts. He is also filled with compassion for the crowd. He knows He cannot leave them unguided. So He began to teach them at great length (Mark 6:34).

What Jesus does with the disciples and the crowd gives us a hint at what He sees to be at the heart of shepherding: compassion. For Jesus, sharing the faith, healing the sick, and preaching the good news, are the shepherd's primary tasks. This is why He is often addressed in the Gospels as Teacher (Matthew 19:16).

In a very special way, this Gospel celebrates what it means to be a compassionate people of faith. Only with Jesus as our shepherd can we call ourselves the people of God. Only when we gather on Sunday in His name, are we what we say we are: God's own people, the flock the Lord tends. That is why our Sunday gathering is so important. It is a necessary expression of our faith, for without the gathering, how are we to be taught? Thus the Lord says: "Whenever two or three are gathered together in my name, there am I in the midst of them" (Matthew 18:20).

Give thought to spend some unhurried time to prepare for church next Saturday or Sunday. Plan ahead so you won't be rushed in getting to church. Come early to get acquainted with the scriptures before the liturgy, and spend some time afterwards to get to know your fellow pilgrims on their journey of faith.

Reflection:

"He pitied them, for they were like sheep without a shepherd; and He began to teach them at great length."

To better understand the above scriptural verse in context, you will find it helpful to read the entire passage: Mark 6: 30–35.

Please reflect on the following:

1. Why is compassion at the heart of the Good Shepherd's teaching? Explain:

   _____

   _____

2. Why is the gathering a necessary expression of faith?

   _____

   _____

   How should you prepare for church?

   _____

   _____

   Give examples:

   _____

3. How important is it to you to be compassionate?

4. Do you feel spiritually nourished when you go to church?

5. What can you do to make your worship in church more meaningful and more compassionate?

6. Prayer:

> I live by Faith
> In the Son of God,
> Who has loved me
> And has given His life for me.
> Grant that I may be faithful to His promise
> And always endeavor to follow Him.

[22] Faith and Vocation

"I called you by name: you are mine."

—*Isaiah*, chapter 43:1

Does a name mean much to you? Well, it does. This is what the Catechism of the Catholic Church has to say about a name:

"God calls each one by name. Everyone's name is sacred. The name is the icon of the person. It demands respect as a sign of the dignity of the person who bears it" (Catechism of the Catholic Church, no. 2158).

There is a story about a Japanese diplomat, Sugihara, who was stationed in Lithuania during the Second World War. He saved thousands of Polish Jews from the Nazis by issuing transit visas to them, defying his own government. Sugihara's bold acts of heroism came to the knowledge of the Israeli government which was gathering names of "courageous rescuers" during the war whose efforts it wished to repay. When Sugihara's valor came to light, Israeli officials immediately made plans to plant a Cherry Grove, as was customary, in the memory of a courageous rescuer. But, in an uncommon move, they rescinded the order and opted for a Cedar Grove, deciding that cedar had holier implications, having been used in the construction of the First Temple.

It was only after they planted the Cedar Grove that the astonished officials learned for the first time that "Sugihara" in Japanese meant: Cedar Grove.

Was it a mere coincidence, do you think, that the name "Sugihara" meant Cedar Grove? Was it mere coincidence also that the Israeli officials changed their plans to plant a Cherry Grove and instead planted a Cedar Grove?

You can never underestimate the importance of a name. Scripture bears witness to this. In the Semitic world, a name was not just a label to identify a person. A name expressed the personality of the person. Take the case of Bartimaeus, mentioned in the Gospel of Mark (Mark 10:46–52). The name of Bartimaeus in Greek meant "son of honor" and this would indicate that Jesus, not only restored the man's sight but his God-given honor as a child of God. The name of Jesus, Joshua in Hebrew, means "Yahweh is salvation;" and the name, Christ, means "the Anointed One." The life of Jesus Christ bore witness to the greatness of His Holy Name. Jesus also emphasized the importance of a name when He changed the name of Simon to Peter, meaning rock, before He appointed him leader of His Church (John 1:42).

Just as we should never take the name of God in vain, we should never disrespect the good name of anyone. As the prophet Isaiah says: "I called you by name: you are mine" (Isaiah 43:1).

Reflection:

"I called you by name: you are mine."

To better understand the above scriptural verse in context, you will find it helpful to read the entire passage: Psalm 43.

Please reflect on the following:

1. Why does scripture set such value in a name?

    Give examples.

    _____

    _____

2. God calls each one by name.

    How do you understand this?

    _____

    _____

3. Name some of the ways a person's good name can be disrespected.

    _____

    _____

4. Praying for someone, even your enemy, shows respect for his or her good name.

    Make a list of those you need to pray for.

    _____

    _____

5. Prayer:

    > Lord God, You have called me by name
    > And have protected me
    > From the snares of the Devil.
    > You permit Evil that Good may come.
    > Listen to my humble prayer
    > For perseverance in times of trial
    > And joy in following the example of Your Son.
    > Amen.

[23] Faith and Comfort

"Come to me, all you who are weary and burdened, and I
will give you rest."

—*The Gospel of Matthew*, chapter 11:28

Let not your heart be weary
Nor your soul be sad
For God is your witness
Upon Him shall you stand.

You have a friend who loves you
Jesus is His name.
Though all else may change
He is always the same.

He is the Alpha and Omega
The beginning and the end
His way is your way
He is your forever friend.

When anxieties burden you
To bring your head down low
Know you can rely on Him
And in His arms let go.

He will pull you close to Him
Where restless strivings cease
He will gather you into His arms
And soothe your soul with peace.

Reflection:

"Come to me, all you who are weary and burdened, and I will give you rest."

To better understand the above scriptural verse in context, you will find it helpful to read the entire passage: Matthew 11:28–30.
Please reflect on the following:

1. Why should you not be weary and burdened?

    Give reasons:

    _____

    _____

2. How does Jesus remain the same while all else changes?

    Give examples from your life experiences.

    _____

    _____

3. What is the meaning of the Alpha and Omega?

    _____

    _____

Why is Jesus the Alpha and the Omega?

_____

_____

4. In what way is Jesus your forever friend?

_____

_____

Jesus calls us to be His friends not His servants.

What is the implication of this calling in your life?

_____

_____

5. This is an age of anxiety.

Jesus not only comforts us but he can remove anxieties from our lives. How has Jesus removed anxieties from your life?

Give Examples:

_____

_____

6.   Prayer:

> If You, oh Lord,
> Should mark our iniquities
> Who could stand it?
> But with You, Lord,
> Is found mercy and healing
> For all those who are weary
> And find life burdensome.

[24] Faith and Community

"Wherever two or three are gathered together in my
name, there am I among them."

—The Gospel of Matthew, chapter 18:20

People like to feel involved and to experience things for themselves. They love to climb Mount Everest if they are up to it;
they like to ascend the Statue of Liberty up to the very torch
itself, tour The White House, see the inside of Air-Force-One, or travel to the Holy Land where Jesus walked. This is, indeed, an admirable
quality and it can be put to good use when it comes to being a community of faith.

If we were to look for the site of the first Christian church of Jerusalem, we would be out of luck. Those first Christians described in the
gospel of Matthew did not have "churches." They were the church,
and their church was a community of faith. They gathered in each other's homes to share the word of the risen Christ. They prayed together;
they shared their earthly goods and property; they shared their meals
after they "broke bread", that is, the Eucharist.

The scriptural notion of "church" is the "gathering" or "assembly"
of believers: "Wherever two or three are gathered together in my
name, there am I among them" (Matthew 18:20). The Church is the
people of God, and the people of God are the Church. This community
of believers is special because its members share a common bond of
faith. This is cause for rejoicing. Faith in the risen Lord leads to "in-
expressible joy touched with glory" (1 Peter 1:8). Why? Because, in

giving expression to your faith in the risen Lord, you are achieving life's spiritual goal: your salvation and the renewal of the world.

Everything Matthew says in chapter eighteen is a portrait of community which we, not only identify with, but in fact are. This is a present-day, historical Church, not of bricks and mortar, not of stained glass or steeples, but of people of faith, anywhere and everywhere throughout the world. It is a portrait of people, who humble themselves; who avoid temptation; who constantly need to be reconciled and forgiven; who pray in the name of Jesus for themselves and for one another. When we see Jesus in the least of our brethren by coming to their aid in times of need, we see the need to be part of a community of faith to help us and support us on our spiritual journey.

There is a great deal of power displayed in this kind of church. This power is the power of the spirit used only as the Lord himself used it: to heal broken bodies and broken hearts, to ignite faith, to loosen purses, to prompt compassion, to encourage a giving kind of love, to feed empty bellies, to support and renew one another; and to give glory to God.

This is what it means to be Church.

Reflection:

"Wherever two or three are gathered together in my name, there am I among them."

To better understand the above scriptural verse in context, you will find it helpful to read the entire passage:

Please reflect on the following: Matthew: 18.1–20.

1. How does a community of Faith describe the Church?

   _____

   _____

2. What is the scriptural notion of Church?

   Give some practical examples:

   _____

   _____

   _____

3. What kind of portrait of Church does St. Matthew offer in chapter 18 of his gospel?

   _____

   _____

4. How is the power of the Spirit displayed in the Church?

   Give examples:

   _____

   _____

5. Prayer:

   Heavenly Father, grant that Your Will
   May be done on Earth as it is in Heaven.
   Whenever two or three gather in the name of Your Son,
   There resides the fullness of the Godhead among us:
   Father, Son and Holy Spirit.

[25] Faith and Light

"For you were once darkness, but now you are light in the Lord."

—Ephesians, chapter 5:8

I n Ghana, in the continent of Africa, many members of a local tribe suffered from blindness. The cause of the blindness, it was discovered, was a mosquito that lived along the river banks and injected a parasite into the bloodstream of local fishermen. To eliminate the blindness, it was necessary to find an antibiotic that would counteract the parasite that was injected into the bloodstream of the fishermen.

Jesus is the antibiotic that eliminates another kind of human blindness; namely, spiritual blindness. In Ephesians, St. Paul, who is writing for Christian converts, equates this blindness to ignorance which is opposed to the will of God (Ephesians 5:17). In fact, Jesus states in John, chapter nine, that he "came into this world for judgment, so that those who do not see might see, and those who do see might become blind." The man, born blind in St. John's Gospel account, chapter nine, was cured of his physical blindness when he professed his faith in Jesus: "I do believe Lord." This twice, fortunate man is an example of those who were "once darkness, but now are light in the Lord" (Ephesians 5:8).

The Pharisees were blinded by their mean-spiritedness because Jesus cured a blind man on the Sabbath. Now, that was really blind of them. They protested: "surely we are not also blind, are we?" But, Jesus let them know that, although they imagined they could see, they were indeed like "blind leaders, leading the blind" (Matthew 15:14).

We need to ask ourselves, in light of today's scripture, what is the fly in the ointment of our lives that blinds us to the truth? Is it ignorance, as St. Paul says; is it pride; is it lust; is it mean-spiritedness; is it hypocrisy; is it idle or irresponsible gossip? What is it? The height of human blindness is to glory in being blind; to reject the truth the same way the Pharisees rejected the miracles of Jesus when He cured people on the Sabbath.

Many people today do not want to see; they have eyes, but they see not; they prefer to tailor the truth to serve their own selfish purposes. The blind Pharisees manipulated the law of the Sabbath to reject the goodness of the Lord. They were blinded by their own self-righteousness.

To see, spiritually, is to be open to the good news of the Gospel and to put it into practice, without being blinded by any form of human selfishness.

Reflection:

"For you were once darkness, but now you are light in the Lord."

To better understand the above scriptural verse in context, you will find it helpful to read the entire passage: Ephesians 5:6–20.
Please reflect on the following:

1. What does St. Paul equate blindness with in Ephesians 5:17?

    Explain:

    _____

    _____

2. What was the blindness of the Pharisees?
    And, how did the blindness of the Pharisees affect others?

    Explain:

    _____

    _____

3. What are the blind spots that are blinding you?
    Make a list of your blind spots:

    _____

    _____

4. Resolve to eliminate from your life whatever is blinding you from being open to the Gospel of Christ.

5. Prayer:

> Proclaim the mighty works of the Lord
> Who has called you out of darkness,
> Into His wonderful light.
> I was lost but now I am found,
> I was blind but now I see.
> His grace has rescued me from darkness
> So I may see clearly through His gift of faith.

[26] Faith and the Eucharist

"Just as the living Father sent me, and I live because of the Father, so whoever eats me will live because of me."

—*Gospel of John*, chapter 6:57

Jesus declares that the bread and the wine of the Eucharist is indeed His body and His blood but He does not explain the process whereby this identity takes place. Why then would Christians, who believe in following Jesus, distance themselves or hate one another because of their disagreements on how He is present in the Eucharist? That is one of the greatest scandals to have plagued Christians for centuries. The disciples of Jesus also had their doubts about the Eucharist. Many of them objected, saying: "This saying is hard; who can accept it?" And, as a result, many of them "returned to their former way of life and no longer accompanied Him" (John 6:60, 66). But, Peter spoke up for the twelve, after Jesus asked them if they also wanted to leave Him, by boldly asserting his faith: "Master, to whom shall we go? You have the words of eternal life" (John 6:60, 67-68). We must remember that the real presence of Jesus in the Eucharist is a mystery. It is not a problem that can be analyzed, studied, and compartmentalized. It is simply a mystery of faith, and the best way to appreciate this mystery is to live it by receiving Christ worthily and by worshiping at the Eucharistic banquet which He has commanded when He said: "do this in memory of me" (Luke 22:19).

The Eucharist is such a rich sacrament that it is the source and the summit of the Christian life. We are all one with the Lord and with one another when we share in the breaking of the bread, the body of

Christ. When we consume the bread and the wine, we are taking Christ into ourselves and we become a living temple in which He tabernacles Himself. Not only is Jesus present everywhere: in creation, in His word, in the community of faith when two or three are gathered together in His name, and in the poor and destitute of the world. He is also present in a particular spot at a particular time when we receive Him into ourselves at holy mass.

Jesus gave us the Eucharist after the miracle of the multiplication of the loaves and fishes (John 6:51-58). His listeners thought it would pay to follow a leader who supplied food in such abundance. But, Jesus had another hunger in mind, another kind of life. And so, Jesus advanced the discussion and focused the interest of His listeners beyond the satisfaction of a full belly to the reception of His very self as our spiritual food under the appearance of bread and wine. At the Eucharist, we accept Jesus's invitation to the meal of salvation. We recognize our own need for repentance, conversion, and reconciliation. We acknowledge our hunger for the Lord. We discover we are bound to one another as we share the same sacred meal together. We also commit ourselves to live according to the teachings of Jesus, and we pledge ourselves to go forth, peacefully, to serve the Lord by satisfying the hunger and thirst of our brothers and sisters in need.

May we all experience the true gift of the Eucharist that unites us to the Lord and impels us to true love and joy around us.

Reflection:

"Just as the living Father sent me, and I live because of the Father, so whoever eats me will live because of me."

To better understand the above scriptural verse in context, you will find it helpful to read the entire passage: John 6:22–71.

Please reflect on the following:

1. Would you describe the presence of Christ in the Eucharist as a mystery?

   ☐ Yes   ☐ No

2. What did St. Peter have to say when Jesus asked the Twelve if they also wanted to leave him because of the Eucharist?

   _____

   _____

   _____

   _____

3. The best way to appreciate the Eucharist is by living it!

   Explain:

   _____

   _____

4. Why did Jesus give us the sacrament of the Eucharist after the miracle of the multiplication of the loaves and fishes?

   Explain:

   _____

   _____

5. Prayer:

   Oh Sacrament most Holy,
   Oh Sacrament Divine.
   All praise and Thanksgiving,
   Be every moment Thine!

[27] Faith and Authority

"What is this? A new teaching with authority."

—*The Gospel of Mark*, chapter 1:27

When Jesus entered the synagogue in Capernaum and began speaking, the people were amazed because he spoke with authority, and not like the Scribes and the Pharisees.

Jesus's authority comes from union with His Father for to know Him is to know the Father (John 14: 7). To know Jesus is also to know the Holy Spirit (John 14: 26) for the Holy Spirit brings to light what Jesus has told us.

What was it about Jesus' preaching, therefore, that was so different? Why were the people so astounded by His message? Why did they say He offered "a new teaching with authority?"

The word 'authority' is derived from the Latin word *auctoritas* and has several meanings: invention, advice, opinion, influence, command or power. People usually associate authority with power, and people in positions of power are said to exercise authority over others by their statements, command, influence or laws. Jesus' authority has the power to change hearts, to comfort the afflicted, and to heal the brokenhearted.

This is why His authority is so different to all other exercises of authority whenever He spoke or acted. He was different to the Scribes; to the Pharisees; to King Herod; to Pontius Pilate. He did not speak like the professional rulers and teachers who quoted from other authorities like the prophets, the Scriptures or Caesar. No, Jesus spoke from the heart, and His words had power to penetrate the heart of His listeners, and bring them to conversion. His words in the Synagogue of Capernaum were so powerful that they drove an evil spirit right out of a man (Mark 1:26).

Jesus changed authority. He freed it from attachment to positions of power. Unlike the rulers of His day, He did not Lord it over others by seeking positions of honor or privilege in Church or State. His authority flowed from the purest truth; the truth He possessed as Son of God. No wonder He could convey His most sublime teaching of the Beatitudes in the simplest way; no wonder He could give us the Lord's Prayer in words that even a child could grasp; no wonder He taught by stories or parables that ordinary people could easily understand.

Jesus changed authority from the exercise of power to service. He came, not to be served but to serve. This is the kind of authority we need to imitate.

Reflection:

"What is this? A new teaching with authority."

To better understand the above scriptural verse in context, you will find it helpful to read the entire passage: Mark 1:21–28.
Please reflect on the following:

1. What is the true meaning of authority?

    Explain.

    _____

    _____

2. How did Jesus change authority?

    Give examples:

    _____

    _____

3. What was the source of Jesus' authority?

    Explain:

    _____

    _____

4. How should Jesus' exercise of authority influence your actions?

Give examples:

_____

_____

5. Prayer:

> Lord Jesus, You taught with the authority
> Not of man but of God.
> At the sound of Your name, every knee
> Should bend, and those in heaven
> And on earth and under the earth,
> And every tongue confess
> That Jesus Christ is Lord,
> To the glory of God the Father.

[28] Living Faith

"Blessed are those servants whom the master finds vigilant on his arrival."

—*The Gospel of Luke*, chapter 12:37

People with no faith often marvel at those who have faith. Some who live by faith seem to get by with little visible means of support. Their support is the invisible God who provides for their every need, who comforts them in times of hardship and leads them safely through life. People of faith have a great gift which no money or influence can buy. Even if you have nothing and still have faith, you have everything. It is more precious than gold or silver or material possessions.

Living by faith asks for a special attitude. It requires you to set your heart on the things of God; on the example of Jesus if you are a Christian; and it calls for specific, daily choices.

Some time ago one of the readers of my blog asked me how I could have faith in a mere theory. In answer, I replied that faith in Jesus, for me, is not a theory. It is a way of life; it affects how I live, how I love and how I treat others. For the Christian, faith in Jesus is very real for He is "the way, the truth, and the life" (John 14:6) who shows us how to live fully.

St. Paul states that faith is "conviction about things we do not see" (Hebrews 11:2). We do not see God but, deep down, we intuit His existence, and sense that He is all around us. We do not see grace but we experience it everywhere, in nature, in the Sacraments of the Church, and in our personal lives when we live by the Gospel. We do not see Jesus with our eyes but we meet Him in others and receive Him in Communion. We do not see the Holy Spirit but we recognize the inspirations of the Holy Spirit when we are moved by the Spirit to follow the dictates of truth. It is because of faith, St. Paul tells us, that men and women of old "were approved by God." Abraham had faith in God, and God blessed him and protected him even when he did not know "where he was going." Sarah believed so strongly that God "was worthy of trust" that she received power to conceive though she was past the age.

What a gift is faith! We lean on this invisible gift when we need help. But, Jesus also asks for a faith that is active and that keeps watch. "Be on guard," He tells us, "like men awaiting their master's return." He asks for the faith that is up and doing, like the servants in Luke, chapter 12. He wants us to treat each other with justice and charity, and to be "vigilant on His arrival." People of faith not only trust an invisible means of support; they are vigilant and visible means of support to others—they are bearers of good news, taking good care of each other.

Our daily lives reflect the gift of faith we bring to each other. It is through our daily experience that we show whether or not we are true servants whom the Master will find "vigilant on His arrival" (Luke 12:37).

Reflection:

"Blessed are those servants whom the master finds vigilant on his arrival."

To better understand the above scriptural verse in context, you will find it helpful to read the entire passage: Luke 12:35–40.

Please reflect on the following:

1. How do you appreciate faith as a gift?

   Give personal examples.

   _____

   _____

2. How has this gift affected your lifestyle?

   Give personal examples.

   _____

   _____

3. "Faith is conviction about things we do not see" (Hebrews, 11:1).

The Trinity lies outside ordinary experience. Can you give other examples of truths of the faith beyond ordinary experience?

_____

_____

4. Prayer:

> Grant us, Lord, the wisdom which You give
> Generously to all without finding fault,
> This wisdom that is from above,
> That is first pure, then peaceful,
> Gentle and reasonable,
> Full of mercy and good fruits,
> Without partiality, without hypocrisy.

[29] Walking by Faith

"Faith is a confident assurance concerning what we hope for, and conviction about things we do not see."

—*Hebrews*, chapter 11:1–2

St. Paul states in his letter to the Hebrews "that faith is a confident assurance concerning what we hope for, and conviction about things we do not see." He then goes on to recount the extraordinary deeds and accomplishments of men and women of faith in the Old Testament. Faith, therefore, is not to be separated from good works. As St. James so well reminds us "faith without good works is dead." St. Augustine, bringing these two aspects of faith together, could say: "faith is believing what you do not see; the reward for this faith is to see what you believe." Faith is more than a notional assent to the good news of the Gospel. For faith to be real, it has to find expression in what you do.

To declare ourselves a people of faith; to be a people who believe in Jesus and in His message; means taking a stand, making a decision. It means deciding that our inner support in life is the good news of the Gospel and then acting on it. To many people, making such a declaration appears too demanding. It seems as overly responsible as the wise virgins in the Gospel story who are pictured wearing their aprons, lighting their lights, and tending the hearth while the master is away (Matthew 25:1–13). Yet, that is precisely what good Christians do. By their daily choices they are saying that their actions are motivated by the good news of Christ, just as surely as if He were there in their midst.

It must be said that a person's faith defines his very self; it describes who he is at the deepest level of his being. Faith is an essential element of life and of living. It is the key to who we are as Christians. More than brains, beauty or brawn, it is faith that gives us drive and direction like the great people of faith St. Paul writes about in Hebrews, chapter eleven.

There is a line from a hymn that says: "we walk by faith, and not by light." This is a kind of theme song for Christians. It doesn't mean that we are stumbling around. In fact it is just the opposite. It means that the path we walk is one of ultimate trust. To walk by faith is to be responsive to the good news of the Gospel, and to the concerns of others; ready to support them on their journey and eager to have them join us on ours.

But, to do this, we need to be people of conviction as St. Paul implies; we need to be convinced that an unseen God who will never forsake us is on our side, guiding and protecting us all the way, in good times and in bad.

Reflection:

"Faith is a confident assurance concerning what we hope for, and conviction about things we do not see."

To better understand the above scriptural verse in context, you will find it helpful to read the entire passage: Hebrews, 1–7.

Please reflect on the following:

1. "Faith without good works is dead" (James 2:17).

   Why is it important that faith find expression in good works or in what you do?

   Give personal examples:

   _____

   _____

   Give examples of faith as good works in the lives of saints or upstanding Christians:

   _____

   _____

2. Did Jesus criticize those who give lip-service to the word without putting it into practice?

   _____

   _____

Give examples in your life of a living, active faith:

_____

_____

3. The wise virgins in the Gospel (Matthew 25:1–13) are examples of those who walk by faith. Why?

_____

_____

4. How does the example of the wise virgins contrast with the foolish virgins in the Gospel?

Give examples:

_____

_____

5. Prayer:

> Our riches, Lord,
> Are the faith that You lit in us.
> Help us to know how to share
> The light of this divine gift
> With those living in darkness,
> Thus establishing for ourselves
> A treasure in heaven.

[30] Faith and Works

"So it is with faith: if it is without works, it is dead."

—*Epistle of James*, chapter 2:17

In this scripture from St. James, we come across an apparent contradiction regarding a truth that is relevant to salvation, one that is so central to the Christian faith that it brought a major split in the Church and still continues to divide some Protestants and Catholics. The apparent contradiction centers on the words of St. Paul in Romans 3:28: "For we hold that a person is justified by faith apart from works prescribed by the law." Martin Luther, who began the Protestant Reformation, understood this as meaning that we are saved by "faith alone." Luther was so convinced of the importance of this viewpoint that he included the word "alone" in his own translation of Romans 3:28, even though it is not in the original text.

How do we reconcile this apparent contradiction between St. Paul's teaching that we are justified by faith apart from works and that of St. James who says that faith without works is dead?

A problem that many Christians today still have is that of confusing justification with salvation. If we keep in mind that God who justified us by faith does not save us by faith alone, we will appreciate that we must bear fruit that results in good works; fruit befitting repentance or the risk of damnation on the last day (see Matthew 7:16–23; John 15:1–2)

The meaning of works is another source of confusion. St. Paul condemns the "works of the law," the slavish adherence to petty rules and regulations without regard to the substantive matters of love and compassion, which led to the attitude of self-righteousness that Christ condemned in the Pharisees (Luke 12:1).

"Works of the law" are actions that are neither morally good nor bad in themselves; because they are performed simply to observe a law. Such actions include keeping the Sabbath, circumcision, and avoiding certain meats.

Good works, on the other hand, are works that are good in themselves because we and others benefit from them; such as, feeding the hungry, clothing the naked, and visiting the sick. We will be judged by whether or not we have practiced these good works on the Last Day: "Whatsoever you do to the least of my brethren, you do to me" (Matthew 25:35–40)

St. Paul explains that works of the law do not bring justification. In no way does he condemn good works which are the result of love. In the Letter to Corinthians St. Paul clearly emphasizes that love is the greatest of the Christian virtues (1 Corinthians 13:13).

The entire Bible is in support of St. James' emphasis on the necessity of faith and good works for Christian living. The account of the Last Judgment given to us in Matthew 25 shows that true faith cannot be separated from good works: "Come, you that are blessed by my Father, inherit the kingdom prepared for you from the foundation of the world; for I was hungry and you gave me food, I was thirsty and you gave me something to drink, I was a stranger and you welcomed me, I was naked and you gave me clothing, I was sick and you took care of me, I was in prison and you visited me... Truly I tell you, just as you did it to one of the least of my brethren, you did it to me" (Matthew 25:34–36, 40).

Let us pray for the conviction then, to translate our faith into good deeds since, as Jesus warns us in Matthew 7:21, "Not everyone who says to me, 'Lord, Lord,' will enter the kingdom of heaven, but only the one who hears my word and puts it into practice."

Reflection:

"So it is with faith: if it is without works, it is dead."

To better understand the above scriptural verse in context, you will find it helpful to read the entire passage: James 2:14–17.

1. What were some of the works prescribed by the law of which St. Paul writes?

_____

_____

   Give examples:

_____

_____

2. What is the difference between works prescribed by the law and good works?

_____

_____

   Give an example of each kind of work:

_____

_____

3. What does the parable on the final judgement in Matthew 25 have to say about good works?

    _____

    _____

    Give examples of good works in Matthew 25, also referred to as the corporal works of Mercy:

    _____

    _____

    _____

4. Prayer:

    Thank you Lord for all the benefits You have given us,
    For all the pains and insults You have borne for us.
    Merciful Redeemer, may we know You more clearly,
    Love You more dearly, follow You more nearly,
    All the days of our lives.

    —Prayer of St. Richard

[31] Ties of Faith

"Whoever does the will of my Heavenly Father is
brother and sister and mother to me."

—*The Gospel of Matthew*, chapter 12:50

T hey say, "You can choose your friends but not your family."
Family is very important in our lives. Without a family to belong to, people would feel rootless; they would be like
directionless ships without sails, especially during the formative years
of childhood. Jesus belonged to a family, and that family nurtured and
protected Him as He matured in wisdom and grace during childhood.

Jesus was addressing the crowds when someone said: "your mother
and your brother are standing out there and they wish to speak to you"
(Matthew 12:57). In the culture of the East, as in Latin cultures today,
the term brothers is often used for cousins, and not necessarily of
brothers in the same family. Jesus replied to the question by asking:
"who is my mother? Who are my brothers?" Then, pointing to his disciples, He said: "there are my mother and my brothers. Whoever does
the will of my heavenly father is brother and sister and mother to me."

What Jesus is talking about here are ties of faith which penetrate a
person's being more deeply than ties of blood. The mother of Jesus
was chosen to be the bearer of the Son of God in the flesh because of
her deep faith, expressed in her words: "thy will be done." A family
whose relationships are grounded in faith, and whose actions are guid-
ed by sound moral and spiritual values, will be a strong family because
those relationships will withstand the seductions of the world, and the

all too human expressions of selfishness that drive families apart rather than pull them together.

Why do we have so many broken families in today's society? Why are there so many divorces? And, why are there so many abandoned and abused children wandering our streets? Family ties; ties of blood; are not enough to bind people together. We need something greater, and that something, the Lord tells us, is doing the will of his heavenly Father. Abraham Lincoln put it beautifully: "My concern is not whether God is on our side; my greatest concern is to be on God's side."

The disciples of Jesus were bound together by the spiritual ties of faith. With the exception of St. John, and St. Paul, they all had wives and, most likely, children. Yet, it was their faith that enabled them to last the course in spite of the persecution and the opposition of a pagan society. It was their faith that bound them together in one mind and one spirit in their love for one another.

Reflection:

"Whoever does the will of my Heavenly Father is brother and sister and mother to me."

To better understand the above scriptural verse in context, you will find it helpful to read the entire passage: Matthew 12:46–50.
Please reflect on the following:

1. Does Jesus denigrate family ties in this scripture?

   _____

   _____

   Why does Jesus put ties of faith above ties of blood?

   _____

   _____

   Give examples of how ties of faith are more important than ties of blood.

   _____

   _____

2. Why is Mother Mary a model of faith for us?

   _____

   _____

Think of someone or some people in your life whose faith has inspired you.

_____

_____

3. Faith is doing the will of your heavenly Father.

   Consider how Jesus did the will of His heavenly Father.

   How can you do the will of your heavenly Father?

   _____

   _____

   Do you do God's will by following the example of Jesus?

   _____

   _____

4. Prayer:

   Lord, in Your great mercy,
   Look kindly upon me.
   In difficult moments,
   Grant that I might not lose heart,
   But remain loyal to Your Son
   Who has shown me
   How to embrace your Holy will.

[32] Faith and the Storms of Life

"He awoke and rebuked the wind and said to the sea: 'Quiet! Be still!' The wind fell off and everything grew calm."

—The Gospel of Mark, chapter 4:39

When storms rage without and within, we often wonder "is God paying attention?' We are so beset with fear that we tend to panic. In this scripture we learn of the son of God calming the raging wind and sea. We learn that God, who created the boundaries of the earth, can remove the crashing seas that threaten us. We are drawn to consider that we are one with the Lord at all times and in times of trouble. This trust in the Lord steadies our ship and brings us peace in spite of troubles.

The apostles faced a mighty storm in this Gospel account, and they became very impatient as they woke the sleeping Jesus, crying out: "doesn't it matter to you that we are going to drown?"

At the command of Jesus, peace came to the turbulent sea and awe fell over the disciples. We can imagine how the apostles' befuddled embarrassment was outstripped by the realization that all heaven opened up in their small sea vessel. Jesus, who had only moments ago slept peacefully on a leather cushion at the stern, brought them to the brink of God's immense world. The apostles appreciated deeper the wisdom of God which is always near to those who trust in Him.

Our world is fraught with difficulties and pitfalls. As Christians we have to navigate through the treacherous waters of life. We have to travel this journey with courage, confidant that Christ is here whether or not we are mindful of Him. God's people cannot expect to slip through life like small sail boats on perfectly glassy seas. The good news is that God is right here, as close as a couple in bed, as yeast in bread or as blood coursing through the veins.

The fishermen of Brittany, before setting out to sea, are accustomed to offer a quiet prayer that is soaked through with faith: "Lord, the sea is so large, and my boat is so small, guide me through these troubled waters." They have learned to lean on the Lord before launching their boats.

Our world, at times, may seem like a lifeboat in troubled waters, which we are desperately trying to hang on to. We need the Lord, in times like that, to calm our souls just as he calmed the disciples on the Sea of Galilee.

Reflection:

"He awoke and rebuked the wind and said to the sea: 'Quiet! Be still!' The wind fell off and everything grew calm."

To better understand the above scriptural verse in context, you will find it helpful to read the entire scriptural passage: Mark 4:35–41.

Please reflect on the following:

1. How does this scripture help you navigate the treacherous waters of life?

_____

_____

Give examples of how your faith helped you to deal with personal struggles.

_____

_____

2. What is the significance of Jesus sleeping peacefully on a cushion at the stern of the boat?

_____

_____

One of the effects of faith is peace. Have you been able to find peace in the midst of trials?

_____

_____

3. God promises to be with us always, in good times and in bad.

   Think of the good times God has been with you.
   Now think of the bad times.

   Have you felt God's presence in both good times and in bad times? Give examples:

_____

_____

4. Prayer:

   Enable us Lord, to dare more boldly,
   To venture on wider seas,
   Where storms will show Your mastery;
   Where losing sight of land,
   We shall find the stars.
   We ask You to push back the horizon of our hopes;
   And to push into the future with faith in You.

[33] Faith and Practice

"Everyone who listens to these words of mine and acts on them will be like a wise man who built his house on rock."

—*The Gospel of Matthew*, chapter 7:24

This Gospel passage challenges us to examine our faith; to discover if we really cherish it and are prepared to put it into practice. "Not everyone who says 'Lord, Lord' will enter the kingdom of heaven, but only the one who does the will of my Father in heaven," asserts the Lord (Matthew 7:21).

Jesus always responded to those who approached Him with faith. He still does.

Faith is not an easy gift to accept. St. Paul makes it clear in Galatians that faith may require taking a stand which is not always popular. He expresses amazement at those Christians who abandoned the true teaching of Christ for "another Gospel." The same thing is happening today. Faith makes demands on us and many people are not up to the challenge. They fall away.

Living the faith is a challenge in today's world. Faith can hardly be called the in-thing today. Faith that is based on the Gospel of Christ involves standards, values, attitudes, beliefs and ways of acting that are counter-culture. Living the faith can mean opposing the popular opinions and ethics of our contemporaries. But, living the faith also means living an authentic life, a life that is transformed by the Gospel of Jesus Christ.

This gift is not given to us by God to be deposited in the misty recesses of the mind. It is something to be exercised and enjoyed, otherwise it will die. There are important ways in which faith is actualized:

1.   Spiritual reading and meditation on the scriptures, such as you're doing now, help to develop the right kind of thoughts in the minds of believers. This is an important way to increase our knowledge of the faith. Prayer is really meditation on the scriptures, and to cultivate a habit of prayer one needs only to ponder the Lord's word in the secrecy of one's heart.

2.   Doing good for someone in need helps to foster the practice of the faith. For example, visiting the sick, the shut-ins and those who are alone in the world; giving a helping hand to needy children, the elderly, the poor in our midst; performing a kind act at home, at school or at work. When you help others in any of these ways you forget about your own problems. Such is the reward of faith.

It is only by living our faith that God and others can respond to us. Faith is like a light, a spiritual light that must shine through what we say and do. This light cannot be left hidden; it must appear for all to see (Matthew 5:16). Only then can we truly delight in it. The sinful woman, who anointed Jesus in St. Luke's account of the event in chapter seven of his Gospel, let her faith shine through (Luke 7:36–50). And, her faith saved her.

The person who listens to the words of scripture "and acts on them will be like a wise man who built his house on rock," says the Lord (Matthew 7:24). This is the faith that saves; this is the faith that imparts peace to believers.

Reflection:

"Everyone who listens to these words of mine and acts on them will be like a wise man who built his house on rock."

To better understand the above scriptural verse in context, you will find it helpful to read the entire scriptural passage: Matthew 7:24–29. Please reflect on the following:

1. How does your faith save you from the false ethics of your contemporaries?

    Give examples:

    _____

    _____

2. Does your faith save you from the errors and false opinions of the day?

    Give examples:

    _____

    _____

3. Are you open to the faith of others who demonstrate it by acts of kindness?

    Consider the many acts of kindness that often go unnoticed by you.

4.   What practical steps can you take to actualize your faith?

Give examples:

_____

_____

5.   Prayer:

Christ with me, Christ before me, Christ behind me,
Christ in me, Christ beneath me, Christ above me,
Christ on my right, Christ on my left,
Christ in the heart of everyone who thinks of me,
Christ in the mouth of everyone who speaks of me,
Christ in every eye that sees me,
Christ in every ear that hears me.

—St. Patrick's Breastplate

[34] Power of Faith

"The Lord replied: if you have faith the size of the mustard seed, you would say this mulberry tree, be uprooted and planted into the sea, and it would obey you."

—*The Gospel of Luke*, chapter 17:5–6

What a thing for Jesus to say! With faith we can uproot trees and have them "planted into the sea." Faith here is a force so powerful that, with it, we can uproot the trees of hatred, prejudice, jealousy, injustice and apathy. Too bad that so many people settle for much less.

The Gospel finds the apostles asking Jesus to increase their faith. Evidently, they realized that faith is a gift and that only through that gift could they accomplish anything worthwhile. Jesus goes on to tell them a story about a master and a servant to underscore the spirit of faith. Keeping the faith is a privilege and a duty. It is not ours to own but to share. It is a gift given to be given again and again. "When you have done all that you have been commanded to do, say: we are useless servants. We have done no more than our duty" (Luke 17:10). How different is this spirit of faith from the spirit of the world!

The spirit of the world is a selfish spirit, a spirit that asks: "what's in it for me?" It is always counting the cost, always looking out for number one, always making demands and always satisfying one's ego and needs. In academic parlance, we call this kind of collective behavior, prescriptive; that is, the perceived needs are set by the general public. This 'modus operandi' may work quite well for the good of all in democratic institutions, provided the sane majority rules and provided a few crafty politicians don't manipulate the process (which usually happens). But, since there is always the danger that the 'innocent' public will be corrupted by the self-serving spirit of selfishness and prejudice our hearts are always yearning for a better spirit. Faith in God alone can rescue us from the spirit of the world and replace it with the spirit of truth.

Faith is a beautiful spirit; it is, as St. Paul states, "no cowardly spirit, but rather one that makes us strong, loving, and wise" (2 Timothy 1:7). Faith does not follow the prescriptive needs of the herd. The needs of faith are normative; that is, they are given, laid down for us in "the rich deposit of faith," in the "sound teaching" of Jesus Christ (2 Timothy 1: 13–14).

No wonder Jesus says, "When you have done all you are commanded to do; say we are useless servants" (Luke 17:10). He is underscoring the spirit of faith and contrasting it with the spirit of the world. The spirit of faith is one of gratitude for the unmerited gift we have received. It is sharing a divine gift that is not ours to own. When people are grateful to God for this power greater than them, they will live by faith and they will deliver results that Jesus compares to moving mountains, and transplanting trees.

Reflection:

"The Lord replied: if you have faith the size of the mustard seed, you would say this mulberry tree, be uprooted and planted into the sea, and it would obey you."

To better understand the above scriptural verse in context, you will find it helpful to read the entire passage: Luke 17:5–10.

Please reflect on the following:

1. What are some of the suffocating roots that the Lord wants to remove from our lives?

   Give examples:

   _____

   _____

2. How is your faith increased?

   _____

   _____

3. Why is sharing your faith so important?

   Give examples.

   _____

   _____

4. Contrast the spirit of faith with the spirit of the world.

   Give examples:

   _____

   _____

5. Prayer:

>   Lord Jesus, I know I am a sinner and
>   I ask for your forgiveness.
>   You died for my sins, and rose from the dead
>   So I might die to sin, and lead a new life.
>   Grant that I may follow You sincerely
>   By loving my brothers and sisters
>   As You have loved me.

[35] Faith and the Trinity

"All that the Father has is mine; that is why I said that the Spirit will take what is mine and show it to you."

—*The Gospel of John*, chapter 16:15

The mystery of the Most Holy Trinity is the central truth of the Christian faith. It is of such cardinal importance that Jesus, not only commissioned His disciples to preach the Gospel to all peoples, but to baptize them in the name of the Father, Son, and Holy Spirit. This truth about the Trinity can be found in chapter 16 of the Gospel of John.

Rather than try to offer a rational explanation of this great mystery, which would be impossible, I will endeavor to describe some of the felt-implications the Trinity can have on our lives.

Firstly, God as Father embraces all of God's children whether they are Catholic, Protestant, Jew, Muslim, Hindu, Buddhist, or Agnostic. As believers in the Fatherhood of God, we are urged to respect and love all peoples irrespective of religious denomination, creed, social origin or background. God as Father reveals himself to us in nature; in the wonderful cycle of the seasons; in the gift of humanity; in the discoveries of the human intellect; in the divine light shining within us which we call—conscience. The Old Testament Bible, which deals with salvation history, recounts the deeds of God the Father for His chosen people, culminating in the Ten Commandments.

Secondly, the second person of the Trinity which we find in the New Testament; namely, Jesus Christ, the son of God, enables the Christian to offer a compelling and practical witness of his or her love of God by following the example of God's only Son. Jesus says: "all that the Father has is mine." Since the Christian believes in Christ, he or she will be impelled to give expression to that belief by example modeled on the life of Christ. To follow Christ is to enlarge our appreciation of the Trinity by relating to each other is a deeply Christ-like way for Christ came into this world to save us from sin and redeem our human nature. He is the way whereby we might love the Father whom we do not see.

Thirdly, the Holy Spirit raises our appreciation of the Trinity to another level. The Holy Spirit has been described by Christ in the Gospels as the spirit of truth (John 16: 13), who will teach us those things that we still must understand about Jesus. The work of the Holy Spirit in the church is progressive and is related to the growth of the people of God in a deeper and more profound appreciation of the Gospel for as Jesus says: "the Spirit will take what is mine and show it to you." We do not know everything there is to know about God because God is a mystery. The Holy Spirit is there to enlighten us whenever the need and occasion arises. This is a wonderful truth, a truth that should make us humble and grateful. The Holy Spirit is working in the people of God in many ways: through the ecumenical movement by creating bridges between different faiths and denominations; through the social and healing ministry of the followers of Christ; and especially through the lives of good Christians who strive to understand Christ's word better and apply it to their lives.

May your life continue to reflect a deeper appreciation of the mystery of God as Father, Son and Holy Spirit.

Reflection:

"All that the Father has is mine; that is why I said that the Spirit will take what is mine and show it to you."

To better understand the above scriptural verse in context, you will find it helpful to read the entire passage: John, chapter 16.

Please reflect on the following:

1. The Most Holy Trinity is a mystery.

    How can it be appreciated?

    _____

    _____

2. What does the Fatherhood of God mean to you?

    Give examples:

    _____

    _____

3. What does God the Son mean to you?

    Give examples:

    _____

    _____

4. What does God the Holy Spirit mean to you?

   Give examples:

   _____

   _____

5. Prayer:

> Oh my God, I firmly believe
> You are one God in three persons,
> And that Your Son became man
> To save us from our sins;
> That You sent Your Holy Spirit
> To help us to do Your will
> On earth as it is in heaven.

[36] Faith and the Incarnation

"The word became flesh and made His dwelling among us, and we saw His glory, the glory as of the Father's only Son, full of grace and truth."

—The Gospel of John, chapter 1:14

Theologians refer to the birth of Christ as the Incarnation, a word derived from the Latin phrase, *in carne,* which means 'in flesh.' The Son of God came down from heaven and took on our lowly nature of flesh and blood. He who is Eternal became bound by space and time; He who is Truth itself spoke in the language of mere mortals; He who is Power itself assumed the powerlessness of a little child. This is a great mystery. The Son of God knew human joy and friendship, sickness and pain, and all that it means to be human. He was subject to human temptation like us and was like us in all things but sin (Hebrews 4:15). Saint John refers to Jesus as 'the Word' (John 1:1), a term he borrowed from stoic philosophy which means 'ultimate reality.' Jesus is the new source of all meaning for every man, woman and child on earth. This meaning which He was born to share with us, is summed up in the word Love; not just erotic love, filial love or mere friendship, but agape, the love that embraces all human beings without distinction, especially the least among us (Matthew 25:40).

The birth of Christ in human flesh is the greatest event if all of history. Not just because the God of Love came to dwell among us as a little child, but because be offers to dwell in us. God is love and we know this, because He sent his Son to show us how to love. True followers of Christ are born of the Spirit, not of the flesh. And the spiritual ties that unite us to Him and to one another are more powerful than ties of blood because they enable us to rise above the daily grind of having to please others, to live by the standards and prejudices of others, or to follow their all-too-human rules and directions. Christ's birth changed all that. His love is so pure that he changed the way we behave and look at life. He entered our world as a helpless child at a time when Caesar, a mere man, was adored as a god and imposed a crippling yoke upon the human spirit. Who among us cannot be humbled by the love of God incarnate (made flesh) in a helpless child who could fit into the palms of your hands? Without an army or legions, without the glitter of a radiant king, this tiny bundle of helplessness lying in a manger has brought us to our senses. He has enlisted more people under his banner than Alexander, Caesar, Genghis Khan, Napoleon, Hitler and Stalin could have ever imagined. His banner is not the banner of might or power, but of love for all humanity. He was born into poverty among animals and a stable was his resting place. His invited guests were mere shepherds; his parents were a single mother and a simple carpenter.

The Incarnation (God made flesh) lives on as long as people of good will walk the walk of Christ, as long as they reject the false values of society, as long as they are kind to one another, as long as they reach out to the needy, the poor and the destitute for whatsoever we do to the least of our brothers and sisters, we give glory to our Father in heaven who sent his Son to be one of us.

Reflection:

"The word became flesh and made His dwelling among us, and we saw His glory, the glory as of the Father's only Son, full of grace and truth."

To better understand the above scriptural verse in context, you will find it helpful to read the entire passage: John 1:1–14.

Please reflect on the following:

1. What does the Incarnation mean?

    Explain:

    _____

    _____

2. St. John uses the Greek term, *logos* (word), to describe Christ.

    What does the Word (*logos*) mean?

    _____

    _____

    Why is it appropriate to apply the term the Word (*logos*), to Christ?

    _____

    _____

3. The ultimate meaning which Christ was born to share with us is summed up in His love. How does the love of Christ (*agape*) fulfill our desire to love one another?

    _____

    _____

4. How does the birth of Christ create a new birth in you?

    _____

    _____

5. Give examples of how your life can be renewed by following Christ.

    _____

    _____

6. Prayer:

    By this we came to know
    The love of God.
    That Christ laid down His life for us
    So we might lay down our lives for one another.
    The Word became Flesh in Nazareth
    And is born again in every human heart
    Who makes room for Him in their lives.

[37] Faith and the Holy Spirit

"He is the one who will baptize with the Holy Spirit."

—*The Gospel of John*, chapter 1:33

The Holy Spirit is sometimes referred to as the forgotten person of the Holy Trinity. A man once remarked to me humorously, when talking about the Holy Trinity: "I can understand God the Father in the Old Testament; and God the Son, in the New Testament; but who is this strange bird they call the Holy Spirit?"

The Holy Spirit is often depicted in paintings as a beautiful white dove with outstretched wings hovering over Jesus, over the apostles, and over the universe. But these creative images do not tell us much about the Holy Spirit. To appreciate the Holy Spirit, we need to read and meditate upon the scriptures.

St. John's Gospel, chapter one, introduces the beginning of Jesus' public ministry just as the ministry of John the Baptist was ending. John the Baptist makes it very clear in this Gospel that his baptism of repentance, which could change outward behavior, was inferior to the baptism of Jesus which could change the person from within. Thus, John the Baptist directed the attention of his followers to Jesus, saying: "He is the one who will baptize with the Holy Spirit."

The Holy Spirit and Jesus are one, just as Jesus and the Father are one. Before He left this earth, the Lord made sure His followers would not be abandoned or left alone. He gave us the Holy Spirit at Pentecost which He referred to by different terms as the Paraclete; the Consoler; and the Spirit of Truth who will guide us and lead us into the fullness of truth.

The Holy Spirit is God's amazing gift-guide us, to help us rise above the limitations of our own human spirit; to help us pray as we should (St. Paul says: "we cannot pray except through the Holy Spirit."); and to help us conquer the "works of the flesh", such as pride, greed, lust, gluttony, jealousy, anger and sloth.

I'm reminded of a conversation between a young Hindu apprentice and a Catholic seminarian. These two enthusiastic students were discussing the merits of their respective faiths. The Catholic pointed out how his faith in Christ and in the good news of the Gospel was able to change the fallen condition of human nature from within; and he proceeded to explain how the eight beatitudes could conquer those attitudes of fallen man (such as pride and greed) that lead to sin. Upon hearing this, the Hindu remarked: "It appears to me that such a change in human behavior would only be possible if you received a new spirit."

The insight of the Hindu student was correct. The Holy Spirit is the new spirit that is given to us to renew our human spirit so that we can pray as Christ shows us; so that we can think as Christ enables us; so that we can see each other as Christ sees us; and so that we can be renewed spiritually to avoid evil and walk freely in the footsteps of the Lord. This is the baptism of Jesus who makes all things new because He renews us from within through the Holy Spirit, the third person of the Most Holy Trinity.

Come Holy Spirit; kindle within us the fire of your love!

Reflection:

"He is the one who will baptize with the Holy Spirit."

To better understand the above scriptural verse in context, you will find it helpful to read the entire passage: John 1:29–34.

Please reflect on the following:

1. Why is the Holy Spirit sometimes viewed as the forgotten person of the Trinity?

   _____

   _____

2. What is the difference between John the Baptist's baptism of repentance and Jesus's baptism of the Holy Spirit?

   Give examples:

   _____

   _____

3. When did the disciples receive the Holy Spirit?

   _____

   _____

4. What are some of the terms used by Jesus to describe the Holy Spirit?

    Give examples:

    _____

    _____

5. Why is the Holy Spirit necessary to pray?

    Give examples:

    _____

    _____

6. Prayer:

    > Come Holy Spirit,
    > Fill the hearts of Your faithful.
    > Enkindle in us the fire of Your love.
    > Send forth Your Spirit
    > That we may be re-created.

[38] Faith and Reason

"In the beginning was the Word, and the Word was with God, and the Word was God."

—*The Gospel of John*, chapter 1:1

The Gospel of St. John, the beloved disciple, is different from the other three synoptic Gospels of Matthew, Mark, and Luke. By the year A.D. 200, St. John's Gospel was called the spiritual Gospel because it tells the story of Jesus in a meditative way that differs sharply from the other three Gospels.

St. John's Gospel was written much later than the other three Gospels and he is the first of the evangelists to incorporate the main philosophical idea of his day into his Gospel. Thus, St. John adopts the notion of the *Logos* (Word) in Stoic philosophy, and applies it to Christ. In Stoic philosophy, the Word signified essential or ultimate reality; and for St. John, this ultimate reality is Christ. He is "the Word" that was "with God," and "was God" (John 1:1)

God has given us two great gifts; the gift of faith and the gift of reason; and it is only right that we use reason to understand faith. This is what St. John does at the beginning of his Gospel; he conveys the Christian teaching about the Incarnation (God made flesh) in the context of contemporary philosophy. There are other theological terms, not found among the literal words of Christ in the New Testament that are accepted within our Christian tradition. Examples of such terms are:

1. Original sin, which is used to explain the Biblical story of mankind's fall from grace.

2. Holy Trinity, which explains the New Testament account of the three persons of the Godhead—Father, Son, and Holy Spirit.

3. Purgatory, a more controversial doctrine as far as some Christian denominations are concerned, which describes the intermediary or Remedial State of preparation before entry into eternal happiness.

We are created as rational beings in the image of God. Everything in the Bible and in the universe has to make sense to be consistent with the Providence of God. Theology, as St. Anselm says, is faith seeking understanding; and this implies using reason to understand revelation. That is why St. John says at the beginning of his Gospel:

"In the beginning was the Word, and the Word was with God, and the Word was God" (John 1:1).

Reflection:

"In the beginning was the Word, and the Word was with God, and the Word was God."

To better understand the above scriptural verse in context, you will find it helpful to read the entire passage: John 1:1–5.

Please reflect on the following:

1. In what way does the Gospel of John differ from the Gospels of Matthew, Mark, and Luke?

   _____

   _____

2. What is the meaning of the term *Word*, in St. John's Gospel?

   _____

   _____

3. Why did St. John use the term *Word*, to describe Christ?

   _____

   _____

4. Christian Tradition uses other terms, not in scripture, to convey the truths of the faith.

Give examples of such terms:

_____

_____

5.   Prayer:

> Your word, Lord, lives among us.
> Lord make me deserving of Your gift of Faith
> Forgive my shortcomings and show me the way
> Endow me with courage to reject temptation.
> Protect me from the envy of others,
> And from my own self interest
> Let me never be parted from You.

[39] Faith and Materialism

"How hard it is for those who have wealth to enter the kingdom of God."

—*The Gospel of Mark*, chapter 10:23

Jesus came on earth to establish a spiritual kingdom, and He calls it the Kingdom of God. Sometimes the term: reign of God, is also used to designate the same concept. This kingdom of God is the antithesis to the kingdom of the world which is ruled by the ambitious, the greedy, and those who are consumed by self-interest and the pursuit of power. In the above quoted scripture, Jesus talks about the greatest obstacle to entering into the kingdom of God; namely, wealth.

During Jesus' time, there was a small gate breaching the walls of Jerusalem that was known as the "eye of the needle." Unencumbered, a person could pass through this gate, but a camel, loaded with goods, was effectively locked out. Only by having its cargo unloaded and getting down on its knees, could a camel be pulled through this gate, known as the "eye of the needle." This striking image of the camel and the needle's eye is presented by Jesus as an example of the burden imposed by riches on those who wish to enter the straight and narrow road that leads to eternal life.

Thus Jesus declares: "How hard it is for those who have wealth to enter the kingdom of God." The rich young man in Mark 10:17–30 who approached Jesus, clearly was seeking the kingdom of God. In fact, his long adherence to the commandments proves as much. Jesus appreciated the young man's good intentions as well as his example of keeping the Commandments. Notwithstanding, Jesus pointed out the impediment to becoming part of God's kingdom: attachment to wealth and riches, but the young man had not the will to lay aside his cargo of material things. Sadly for the young man, Jesus revealed how this burden would bulge and bloat to the size of a camel and block his way into God's kingdom.

This story of the rich young man who was attached to wealth and money is true of many people today. Wealth is relative, and it is the attachment to wealth that Jesus condemns. If you put your trust in wealth and material things, no matter how large or small, before your devotion to Christ, you will be like the rich young man in today's Gospel.

Everyone has an Achilles' heel, a weakness, a little vice, a prized possession that burdens us and keeps our hearts from being open to receive the gift of God's Kingdom. We must rid ourselves of these obstacles in order to enter, childlike, into God's realm. Attachment to materials things could be as simple as attachment to a car or as complex as attachment to a yacht, a mansion or a business. These are only things at the end of the day and in no way compare to the respect and honor due to Almighty God.

Whatever it is in your life that prevents you from accepting the Gospel —whether it is money, a car, your business, your career know that it is dulling you and tarnishing your spirit. Let God gift you, and like grateful and open minded people, escape from the hold of material possessions and enter into the kingdom of light.

Set yourself free!

Reflection:

"How hard it is for those who have wealth to enter the kingdom of God."

To better understand the above scriptural verse in context, you will find it helpful to read the entire passage: Mark 10:17–31.

Please reflect on the following:

1. How is the Kingdom of God different to the Kingdom of the world?

   Give examples:

   _____

   _____

2. Why did the rich man's wealth become an obstacle to entering the kingdom of God?

   _____

   _____

3. Is Jesus opposed to wealth or to attachment to wealth?

   Explain:

   _____

   _____

4. From what material attachments should you free yourself?

   Make a list:

   _____

   _____

   _____

   _____

5. Prayer:

   May we never boast
   Except in the Cross of Christ.
   For the wood of the Cross is God's saving power.
   May we have the strength to reject
   The principalities and powers of this world:
   The lure of wealth and boast of power
   Which await their inevitable end
   Like dust scattered in the wind.

[40] Faith and Prayer

"Jesus told his disciples a parable about the necessity for them to pray always without becoming weary."

—*The Gospel of Luke*, chapter 18:1

S ome people imagine that prayer comes forth spontaneously from an overflowing heart, and surmise that if the heart does not start to pray by itself they can never pray. Such a notion is just wishful thinking. It is true that forced prayer is no prayer, but it is also true that prayer, like any heart-felt activity of value, demands effort.

For people of faith, prayer is an essential part of their being. It is a spiritual lifeline: a means of contact with the Father in Heaven. It can be as simple as a good thought; and as magnificent as raising your mind to contemplate God's will for you. It is an activity that you can always engage in whenever you reach out to someone in friendship. Whether you are standing or sitting or walking or driving your car, prayer is a matter of the heart, a heart that rests in God.

You do not have to be an articulate speaker to pray. Our stammerings are all accepted and understood by a generous God who knows the secrets of our hearts (Romans 8: 26). No matter the confusion of your mind or heart; no matter how awkwardly you reach for words; God listens lovingly as a parent listens to children. Whenever you sit down or kneel down to pray, know that it is natural for the distractions of this world to swirl around in your mind and intrude into your prayers. What should you do? Don't give up. Rather, ask the Lord to take away your distractions; let them go. Be not discouraged, and never lose heart because the Holy Spirit will guide you.

The parable Jesus shared with his disciples in chapter eighteen of St. Luke's Gospel about a widow and a dishonest judge underscores the importance of not losing heart or giving up when you pray. The dishonest judge in this parable granted the widow's request because of her persistence. "Will not God," Jesus says, "secure the rights of his chosen ones who call out to him day and night?" (Luke 18: 7).

Some people also wonder why we have to ask God to answer our prayers. Does not God already know what we want even before we ask Him? Did Jesus not say, "when you pray, go into your room, lock the door; and your Heavenly Father, who knows your needs, will grant them in secret?" (Matthew 6: 6). So, why ask God to answer your prayers?

God respects our free will and He wants us to have a trusting relationship with Him. He wants us to ask Him to answer our prayers, like a good parent who would say to a child who needed something, "why didn't you ask me; don't you know I would have given it to you." Jesus wants us to pray to the Father, in His name, through the Holy Spirit. Whatever we ask for in Jesus's name will be granted to us (John 14: 13).

Many people go to Church on Sunday out of routine, never really listening to the words they hear in the scriptures. Their minds can be on something else: a movie, bills to pay, tiresome neighbors. It is only when they awaken to the message of the scriptures that they begin to understand its power to liberate them from the grind of daily living. This awakening normally happens when a person is plunged into a personal crisis, and feels the need to delve deeper into the scriptures in search of meaning. I have been approached by individuals who told me they attended mass for years without ever really listening to the scriptures. When they finally opened their minds to the scriptures like the two disciples on the way to Emmaus (Luke 24: 13–35), the difference that was wrought in their lives was life-changing.

The lesson in today's scripture is: if you do not ask, you will not receive. Even though the Lord knows what you need before you pray; He wants you to ask; He wants you to pray without ceasing because He loves you as your Father.

And, as your Father in Heaven, He is eager to grant the prayers of his chosen ones.

Reflection:

"Jesus told his disciples a parable about the necessity for them to pray always without becoming weary."

To better understand the above scriptural verse in context, you will find it helpful to read the entire passage: Luke 18:1–8.

Please reflect on the following:

1. Why is prayer an essential part of a Christian's being?

   _____

   _____

2. Is the Holy Spirit necessary to pray?

   Why?

   _____

   _____

3. Prayer is meditation on the scriptures.

   Explain the reason why:

   _____

   _____

4. Prayer is more than Church attendance.

    Explain why this is so:

    _____

    _____

5. How is it possible to pray always?

    Give examples:

    _____

    _____

6. What will you do to cultivate a prayerful life?

    Set some goals for yourself:

    _____

    _____

    _____

    _____

    _____

    _____

7. Prayer:

> God grant me the ability
> To live one day at a time.
> To accept hardships as the way to peace,
> To take as Jesus did this sinful world
> As it is, not as I would have it.
> To trust that His Providence will make all things right,
> If I but surrender to His will,
> So that I may be content in this life,
> And happy with Him in the next.

[41] Faith and Eternal Life

"God so loved the world that He sent His only begotten Son that whoever believes in Him might not perish but have eternal life."

—Gospel of John, chapter 3:16

The gift of eternal life was lavished upon us through the death and resurrection of Jesus Christ. "I have come that you may have life," says the Lord, "and have it in abundance" (John 10:10). All human life and the life of nature will come to an end, but the Lord's gift of eternal life will last forever. This truth of faith is beautifully depicted over the triple doorways of the famous Cathedral of Milan, Italy.

Over one is carved a beautiful wreath of roses, and underneath it is the caption: "All that which pleases is but for a moment." The wreath of roses represents all that is beautiful and enjoyable about life, but in the end that too will pass. In comparison with eternal life, it is but a passing attraction.

Over the other is sculptured a cross, and there are the words, "All that which troubles us is but for a moment." It is important to realize that nothing lasts forever. Whatever is troubling you right now will pass and be no more. So, why worry and fret your life away over anxieties that will pass and be forgotten? In time, you will not even remember what it was that upset you in the past. Time, it is said, is a great healer. The Lord does not call you to be perfect and without blemish. He calls you to be faithful; to follow Him and accept His gift of eternal life.

Underneath the great central entrance to the main aisle is the third inscription, "That only is important which is eternal." We are living in a world of appearances, of passing things, and the only thing that will satisfy our cravings is that which is permanent and eternal. Our lives are a journey, and our hearts will be restless unless they find comfort in the source and summit of our being: the Lord God Almighty who created us. "Come to me all you who labor and are burdened," says the Lord "and I will refresh you."(Matthew 11: 28)

If we always realize these three truths, we will not let trifles trouble us, nor be interested so much in the passing pleasures of the hour that cannot give lasting joy. We should live for what will last, but enjoy the moment.

This reminds me of a story when a visitor to Africa came to call on a priest. He was appalled at the appearance of the priest's living quarters which only had the bare necessities of life. He asked the priest, "Father, why are you living in such sparsely furnished quarters? Do you need funds so badly?" The priest answered by asking, "Why are you traveling so lightly?" The guest answered, "But I am just a visitor here." "So am I" the priest answered.

Let us remember that we are all 'visitors' here and we should prepare ourselves to live the new life that Jesus came on earth to give us so that we can possess it forever in the next life.

Reflection:

"God so loved the world that He sent His only begotten Son that whoever believes in Him might not perish but have eternal life."

To better understand the above scriptural verse in context, you will find it helpful to read the entire passage: John 3:16–21.

Please reflect on the following:

1. Jesus bestows the gift of eternal life to those who believe in Him.

    How would you describe eternal life?

    _____

    _____

2. What does the first inscription over the doorway of the Cathedral of Milan say?

    _____

    _____

    How do you interpret this inscription?

    _____

    _____

3. What does the second inscription over the doorway say?

_____

_____

What does this inscription mean?

_____

_____

4. What does the final inscription say

_____

_____

What does it mean?

_____

_____

5. Prayer:
   God loves us, and we know this
   Because he sent His Son to redeem us.
   In nothing, therefore, be anxious but in everything,
   By prayer and petition with Thanksgiving,
   Let your regrets be made known to God.
   And the peace of God which surpasses all understanding.
   Will guard your hearts and your thoughts.
   In Christ Jesus.

[42] Faith and Purgatory

"Then Peter said: Lord: is this parable meant for us or for everyone?"

—The Gospel of Luke, chapter 12:41

Peter asked Jesus if the parable He just recounted was for the disciples or for everyone? It is obvious that this parable about the Faithful and Unfaithful servants (Luke 12:41–48) was for everyone. Jesus imparts here a lesson for all of us about faithfulness, and He offers three different images of His servants during His absence.

The first group is the wise followers or servants who remain steadfast, doing their duty even in the master's absence. The next two groupings are the foolish servants who adopt a complacent lifestyle during the master's absence, thus abusing their positions of responsibility. The day of reckoning, however, comes when the master returns.

The faithful servants receive their reward (Luke 12: 43).

The unfaithful servants are treated differently according to the level of their failure to do the Master's will, and they are divided into two categories:

1. Those who are "punished with a heavy beating" (Luke 12:46–47).
2. Those who are "punished with a light beating" (Luke 12:48).

We should all be familiar with the two groups of followers of Jesus in Matthew 25:31–46, who will be separated on judgment day—the sheep on the right and the goats on the left; the faithful and the unfaithful. But what is this extra group that Jesus now talks about in today's Gospel, Luke 12:48, who will receive "a light beating?" This is not the blessed group in heaven for they will receive no beating at all. And, it is different to the group who will receive a "heavy beating," (Luke 12:46–47) and be condemned to "eternal punishment" (Matthew 25—26).

Today's parable introduces the theological notion we call Purgatory that leads us to the realization that, besides heaven and hell, there is an in-between state of remedial punishment; the "light beating" which Luke talks about. The Church's tradition, based on this New Testament scripture, as well as references in the Old Testament, upholds the doctrine of a state of temporary, remedial punishment for believers who die in venial sin (otherwise known as Purgatory). Believers who are committed to purgatory, cannot be admitted to Heaven immediately or directly because they have guilt and yet they cannot be consigned to "eternal punishment" in Hell because their sin is not mortal (1 John 5:16–17). Many Christians have a problem with this doctrine of purgatory. One reason for this is that the Reformation Bible does not include the book of Maccabees 2 which supports this doctrine. The doctrine of purgatory makes sense, especially in light of today's scripture, which provides a third alternative to outright blessing and outright condemnation on the Day of Judgment.

The parable of the Faithful and Unfaithful servants graces us with God's mercy as well as God's justice. Purgatory is good news for all of us and for all our struggling brothers and sisters who never quite seem, in this life, to measure up to the Gospel of Christ. It is a great source of hope to know that even if we die in an imperfect state, we can still be purified, and will only receive "a light beating" before being admitted to eternal happiness.

Let us pray for the poor souls in Purgatory who are awaiting everlasting happiness in Heaven.

Reflection:

"Then Peter said: Lord: is this parable meant for us or for every-one?"

To better understand the above scriptural verse in context, you will find it helpful to read the entire passage: Luke 12:41–48.
Please reflect on the following:

1. What are the three types of servants mentioned by St. Luke in the parable of the Faithful and Unfaithful servants?

    Give examples:

    _____

    _____

2. How many types of Faithful and Unfaithful servants are men-tioned in Matthew 25 (The parable of the last judgment)?

    Give examples:

    _____

    _____

3. Why does the doctrine of purgatory make theological sense in this parable in Luke 12:41–48?

    _____

    _____

4. Explain how this parable joins God's mercy with His justice.

    _____

    _____

5. Prayer:

> Lord, we are all Your children,
> And Your blessings are everywhere to be found.
> May You bless us and keep us.
> Make Your Face shine upon us,
> And be gracious to us.
> Lift up Your countenance upon us
> And give us Your peace.

[43] Faith and Passion

"I have come to set the earth on fire, and how I wish it were already ignited!"

—*The Gospel of Luke*, chapter 12:49

The Christian Gospel is primarily a way of life, not a theory. It offers new life, and is convincing, primarily, as witness. The evidence of Christianity is shown by the good example, the change-for-the-better which it is capable of producing in people's lives. On this it either stands or falls. Faith must be shown to make sense even if it is a mystery. Theologians can demonstrate that faith does not contain internal contradictions, that it does not contradict scientific knowledge. The proof of faith, the worthwhileness of faith, however, can only be demonstrated by showing the real and practical evidence of its value; the evidence of a new spirit (the Holy Spirit) in our lives.

Today's scripture is indeed a call to war; a non-violent war; not a war against other people but a war against sin and corruption; not a war against people whom we perceive as evil, but a war against evil itself. Hardly a day passes that we do not hear the sad news of violent aggression and brutality against innocent people somewhere around the world. To make matters worse, some perpetrators of these violent acts justify them by claiming they are fighting a holy war in God's name. Think of the Taliban in Afghanistan; ISIS in Syria; Boco Haram in Africa; and several other fanatical, politico-religious groups.

The inevitable consequence of Jesus's message is to put the children of God in opposition to worldly evil, not in a violent way but non-violently according to the example of Jesus. This is the fire that Jesus wants to ignite in us in order to purify the world of evil. This is the perpetual conflict between the Christian and the forces of evil which the New Testament says can exist under the same roof among our family members (Luke 12: 53), in our neighborhoods, and within ourselves (Romans 7: 23).

Jesus wants to change the way we look at the world, the way we live, work and die. The true follower of Christ regards his life in this world, not simply as a series of earthly happenings, but as being vitally related to God's Providence. The Christian takes it for granted that there is a constant interplay between nature and grace, that there is something above and beyond the world of nature and events that manifests the presence of God. What may be a religious experience for one may not be a religious experience for another. The starry heavens above, the shining splendor of the Milky Way, may be viewed as a distant amalgam of atomic phenomena by a non-believer. To the Christian, however, these are not only marvelous wonders of nature; these are the handiwork of God.

Jesus came on earth to set it on fire with a new spirit, and a new message of love for all humankind. Those who engage in this mission can expect opposition from their enemies: the children of this world, who have much to lose, and who will not give up easily. Jesus did not escape suffering and death at the hands of His enemies.

The good news is that Jesus, who has overcome the evil of the world, will never forsake those who follow Him with conviction and passion.

Reflection:

"I have come to set the earth on fire, and how I wish it were already ignited!"

To better understand the above scriptural verse in context, you will find it helpful to read the entire passage: Luke 12:49–53.

Please reflect on the following:

1. Why does Jesus say He wants to set the earth on fire?

_____

_____

Give examples of the struggle between grace (the Gospel) and the forces of evil.

_____

_____

2. The Gospel is primarily a way of life.

    Explain how this is the case.

_____

_____

3. Each Christian is engaged in a non-violent war against the forces of evil.

   How is this kind of struggle to be conducted?

   _____

   _____

4. Prayer:

   > Lord, make me passionate in my Faith.
   > Enable me to share it with whomever I meet
   > By example rather than with words.
   > May the fire of Your message burn in my heart
   > So that I may be a beacon of light to those in darkness
   > And a comfort to those in distress.

[44] Faith and Forgiveness

"Whose sins you shall forgive, they are forgiven."

—*The Gospel of John*, chapter 20:23

Teilhard de Chardin, the Jesuit paleontologist and geologist who took part in the discovery of Peking Man, once remarked that it is extremely difficult to locate the original of a great many ordinary things: the first flat iron, toaster, teapot, etc. Much the same could be said of "Confession," as we practice it, with its image of an anonymous penitent in a small dark box, telling his or her sins to a priest and receiving absolution. We know from today's scripture that Jesus gave the power to forgive sins to His church, but we search in vain for the original of this practice in the early centuries of Christianity.

What we do find is something called public penance. Once in their lifetime, sinners who had shocked the community by their behavior could be brought back to the community, but only by the bishop and only after a lengthy period of public penance. Where then, did private "confession," as we know it, come from?

Apparently, it owes its origins to Irish Monks. When Christianity came to that western island, it quickly took on a monastic tone, and monks adapted an old pagan custom, that of the counselor friend ("soul friend" or, in Gaelic, *Anamchara*.) The counselor friend would search out the scars that sin had left in the other's life. If a sinful pattern of behavior needed to be changed, the counselor friend would pray to God for forgiveness and the penitent would resolve to improve his or her life. This was the monk's "confession," and it became a venerable vehicle for spiritual development.

The practice proved popular with the lay people who lived in the monastery surroundings and they began making their "confession" to the monks. As time went by, it became the function of the priest to reconcile the sinner to the community by imparting absolution.

When the Irish monks poured across Europe on their missionary journeys during the Dark Ages after the fall of the Roman Empire, they took the practice of private Confession with them. For some time, various synods of bishops were uneasy with the idea of Confession, repeatable and easily accessible as it was. They attempted unsuccessfully to cling to the ancient practice of public penance. But private Confession was an idea whose time had come. It soon became the accepted pattern for reconciling the sinner and it, eventually, received the church's full endorsement.

The practice of slipping quietly into a confessional, whispering one's sins anonymously to an unknown priest and then receiving absolution, appealed more strongly to people than the severe penitential discipline of the early church.

Today, in the Catholic Church, especially after the Second Vatican Council (1962–1965), the Sacrament of Confession or Penance has undergone new developments. The Penitent now has a choice:

1. To confess anonymously one's sins to an unknown priest in the confessional box.
2. To confess one's sins, face to face with the priest at a regularly scheduled time or by appointment.

Both these options are available to all parishioners in every parish throughout the world.

Some people tend to portray Confession as a convenient and easy way of receiving forgiveness without being accountable for one's sins. This is a grave misunderstanding of this sacrament. Confession, to be authentic, must possess the following:

1. Sorrow for one's sins: A person requesting the Lord's forgiveness in Confession must be truly sorry for sins committed.

2. Sincere purpose of amendment: A person requesting the Lord's forgiveness must be ready to make amends for the sin or sins committed and resolve not to repeat them.

3. Act of penance: A person requesting the Lord's forgiveness must do some sort of penance for sin. The priest, during Confession, assigns an appropriate penance.

The above requirements are necessary for a good Confession. The priest, who exercises Christ's ministry of forgiveness, then imparts absolution in the name of the Father, and of the Son, and of the Holy Spirit.

Reflection:

"Whose sins you shall forgive, they are forgiven."

To better understand the above scriptural verse in context, you will find it helpful to read the entire passage: John 20:19–23.

Please reflect on the following:

1. Describe the ancient practice of Public Penance:

_____

_____

Who restored the penitent to the community according to the ancient practice of Public Penance?

_____

_____

2. How did the present practice of Private Confession come about?

_____

_____

How did it differ from the ancient practice of Public Penance?

Give examples:

_____

3. Since the Second Vatican Council, Confession has undergone new developments.

   What are the two choices now open to the penitent?

   _____

   _____

4. What are the three requirements for a good confession?

   _____

   _____

5. Prayer:

   > Lord, You are patient with sinners
   > And accept our desire to make amends.
   > I acknowledge my sins
   > And I am resolved to change my life.
   > Grant me the strength to admit my shortcomings
   > And be renewed by the power of Your Gospel.

[45] Faith and Repentance

"I have come not to call the righteous to repentance, but sinners."

—*The Gospel of Luke*, chapter 5:32

We all need to repent. In the Old Testament we are told that "the just man sins seven times a day" (Proverbs 24:16). If we are honest with ourselves we will discover that many of our actions are tainted with some degree of sin or selfishness. Even our pursuit of God's kingdom is not always pursued with the best of intentions. How many are prepared to live exemplary lives just to please God without regard for one's own self-interest? Many of today's televangelists make a successful business of religion but are they as enthusiastic in making it their business to imitate and promote the selfless example of Christ in their lives? How many scandals in the Church could be avoided if only "religious' people were more truthful and more honest in their commitment to the Gospel?

Jesus was surrounded by sinners who knew and admitted they were sinners. These were the good people because they were not hypocrites; they knew they were missing the mark and they were open to change. The Sinner and the Saint both have something special in common: they know they are sinners. The difference is that the Saint was able to overcome the downward pull of sin, and accept the upward pull of grace.

A Saint like the lovable St. Patrick, the patron of Ireland, was not afraid to acknowledge he was a sinner. In fact, he began his Confessions with these simple words: "I Patrick, a sinner..." He was truthful and, like all the great saints, he could accept this reality whenever he saw others stumble: "there go I but for the grace of God."

Jesus was also surrounded by many sinners who refused to recognize they were sinners. These were the bad people, the self-righteous ones, and the hypocrites who criticized Jesus for eating with sinners (Luke 5:30). They were too blind to see that they were no different from anyone else. Thus they could not reform their lives because they thought of themselves as perfect. It is important for us to acknowledge that, although we are called to holiness of life, we are always imperfect pilgrims on a journey which can only reach fulfillment in Heaven. We are called, in this life, to be faithful, not perfect. My dear mother used to tell me when I was a child and prone to get out of hand: "The Saints are in Heaven, and you, my son, have a long way to go and much to learn before God is finished with you."

Jesus says in today's scripture, "I have come not to call the righteous to repentance, but sinners." He sent a powerful message to the Pharisees and to the Scribes who criticized Him for dining with tax collectors when he called Levi, a tax collector, to follow Him (Luke 5:27–32). Let us never forget that we are sinners in need of repentance. Jesus is our spiritual doctor who provides us with the spiritual cure. Let us begin by acknowledging our need to be cured; to repent of our sins. When a person thinks he has no need of repentance, he is, surely, the sickest of all.

Jesus loved the sinner, and never ceased to show him or her His compassion and mercy. His most touching stories are about those who strayed from the right path—the Prodigal Son; the woman caught in adultery; the Samaritan woman at the well; St. Peter who denied Him; St. Thomas who doubted Him. The list goes on and on. All these stories have one thing in common; they all show the power of repentance to turn one away from sin and to become a new person.

Reflection:

"I have come not to call the righteous to repentance, but sinners."

To better understand the above scriptural verse in context, you will find it helpful to read the entire passage: Luke 5:27–32.

Please reflect on the following:

1. Is everyone in need of repentance?

    Give examples:

    _____

    _____

2. Why did Jesus love the sinner?

    Give examples of Jesus's love of sinners.

    _____

    _____

3. Why was Jesus opposed to the self-righteous attitude and behavior of the Pharisees?

    _____

    _____

Give an example from today's Gospel message.

_____

_____

4. Who was the tax collector Jesus called to be His disciple in today's Gospel?

_____

_____

5. What sins are you in need of repentance?

_____

_____

6. Prayer:

> We are saved, Lord, not by being righteous,
> But by trusting in Your mercy and goodness.
> We are all in need of repentance
> Because we are all sinners.
> And none of us are righteous.
> Grant that we who trust in Your mercy
> Shall receive Your blessing of forgiveness.

[46] Faith and Worship

"The hour is coming... when authentic worshippers will
worship the Father in spirit and in truth."

—*The Gospel of John*, chapter 4:23

I n the minds of the people of Jesus' time, the temple had come to
be identified with the place where authentic worship of God took
place. The average worshiper saw nothing amiss in having animals and coins set aside for sacrificial use within the temple. Jesus,
however, had a different appreciation of worship. In an extraordinary
encounter between Jesus and a Samaritan woman at a well, Jesus
makes it clear that the Father seeks out those who will worship, not on
a mountain (as the Samaritans worshiped) or in the temple (as the
Jews worshiped) but in spirit and in truth (John 4:4–26).

Worship in spirit and in truth goes deeper and beyond the confines
of the temple and places of worship. This is not to say that places of
worship are not important. What is clear from the words of Christ is
that true, lasting worship takes place in the heart; in your inner temple
through the workings of the Holy Spirit. St. Paul beautifully elaborates
on this teaching of faith when he declares: "Do you not know that
your bodies are temples of the Holy Spirit, who is in you, whom you
have received from God?" (1 Corinthians 6:19). Christians are a people of the Most Holy Trinity. It is God the Father who created our
bodies; God the Son who redeemed them; and it is God the Holy Spirit who indwells them.

Jesus identifies Himself as the living temple. What Jesus did when
he knocked over the money changers' tables was to indicate a drastic

shift in what it means to worship God and to be in His presence (Matthew 21: 13). Jesus replaced the temple as the focus of worship with Himself. He referred to Himself as the new temple which could not be destroyed. "Destroy this temple," was Jesus' answer, "and in three days I will raise it up" (John 2:19).

The only way we can be in relationship with God is to worship in an entirely new way. To be one with God is to be one with Jesus. The commandments, in themselves, are not the whole will of God for us. We cannot base our spiritual life on the commandments alone. To do so would be to delude ourselves into thinking that God's will for us is contained only in the law. But we are not justified by works of the law (Galatians 2: 16). Living only legally can lead to great acts of inhumanity. Such inhumanity led the Pharisees to condemn Jesus to death; it enabled them to have a woman caught in adultery stoned to death. Jesus did not abrogate the commandments. Rather, He placed them in a new light: the light of the eight beatitudes that backtrack to the condition of the human heart. The person and example of Jesus is the sign of the new covenant. The eight beatitudes, which He has given us, are the blueprint for Christian worship in spirit and in truth. By following Jesus's example, our worship is perfected in spirit and in truth.

The new and authentic worship of Jesus takes place in the heart where the Holy Spirit wishes to dwell (Proverbs 20: 27). This new worship starts with a change of attitude which lets go of anger, pride, envy, greed and different forms of human selfishness. The Christian beatitudes of humility, compassion, meekness, purity of heart, patience, peacefulness and generosity give witness to authentic worship in spirit and in truth, and you can carry it with you wherever you go.

Reflection:

"The hour is coming... when authentic worshippers will worship the Father in spirit and in truth."

To better understand the above scriptural verse in context, you will find it helpful to read the entire passage: John 4:4–26.
Please reflect on the following:

1. How is worship in spirit and in truth different to temple worship?

_____

_____

Give examples:

_____

_____

2. Why did Jesus identify Himself as the Living Temple?

_____

_____

Give examples of how Jesus personalized worship.

_____

_____

3. Why are the Beatitudes of Jesus the blueprint for Christian worship?

_____

_____

Give examples.

_____

_____

4. Worship in spirit and in truth can travel with you wherever you go.

Explain:

_____

_____

5. Prayer:

> Lord, You instruct us
> That the Kingdom of God is within us,
> And our bodies are temples of the Holy Spirit
> Wherein true wisdom lies.
> Grant that we may enter this inner temple,
> A place of meditation
> Where true worship takes place
> In spirit and in truth.

[47] Faith and God's Will

"Thy will be done on earth as it is in Heaven."

—The Gospel of Matthew, chapter 6:10

All of God's creation is sacred even if we live in a world that tends to denigrate His sovereignty over nature. Grace builds on nature, and Jesus came on earth, "not to destroy but to fulfill" (Matthew 5:17). He did not come to condemn the world; rather, He came to save the world, and those who live in it (John 3:17).

Jesus had a full life. He went to wedding parties, and at one such party He changed water into wine. He had all kinds of friends; politicians, tax collectors, widows, traitors, divorcees, saints and sinners. At no time, did Jesus ration His gift of the spirit (John 3:17). He reached out to everyone; the poor, the lame, the blind, the wealthy, tax collectors, synagogue officials, and a Roman Centurion. He called simple fishermen to be His disciples, and empowered them to be His witnesses after His death and resurrection. He calls us too to be His followers and shows us what it means to do God's will on earth as it is in heaven.

Doing God's will brings with it an awareness of our human need to grow according to His higher purpose in our lives. Jesus enables us to be renewed in the spirit; to be forgiven of our sins; and to walk in the newness of His example. Through Him, we can forget our sins, confident in His unconditional forgiveness. Like St. Paul we need give "no thought to what lies behind, but push on to what is ahead" (Philippians 3:13).

Knowing God's purpose for us is our greatest asset in life. The faith to know this is God's gift to us. It is not a reward for anything we have accomplished. So let us never pride ourselves on our accomplishments like the self-righteous Pharisee who boasted about his achievements, while condemning the poor publican who was praying in the temple (Luke 18:11).

We need to ask the Lord, daily, for the wisdom to do His holy will. As you do this, you will possess the freedom of the children of God who acknowledge that He is in charge because it is God's will that matters, not your own.

Jesus came into this world to show us how to do God's will. The history of mankind testifies that the human race hasn't done a good job of pursuing God's higher purpose on earth. So, when we pray, we should recognize that " we do not know what to pray for as we ought" (Romans 8: 26) for God's will and our will often clash whenever we pray for things opposed to our salvation. Thus we are often denied the things we ask for by Him who knows what is best for us.

When we pray: 'Thy will be done,' we are praying that God will use us to do His holy will. 'Thy will be done' was the prayer of Mary after it was revealed to her that she would become the bearer of Christ. It was the prayer of Jesus in Gethsemane after He prayed thrice to escape His suffering: "Not my will, but thine be done" (Matthew 26:39, 42).

'Thy will be done' should not be interpreted as resignation, fatalism, defeatism, or slavish acceptance of the status quo. When we make this beautiful prayer (the third petition of the Our Father) we are praying that God's love and peace will become a reality in our lives; and that God will give us the grace and perseverance to stay the course to fight the good fight as a faithful follower of His only begotten Son.

Reflection:

"Thy will be done on earth as it is in Heaven."

To better understand the above scriptural verse in context, you will find it helpful to read the entire passage: Matthew 6:9–15.
Please reflect on the following:

1. What does God's will mean to you?

———————————————————————

———————————————————————

Give examples:

———————————————————————

———————————————————————

2. Does God call everyone to do His will?

———————————————————————

———————————————————————

Give examples of the different kinds of people He calls.

———————————————————————

———————————————————————

3. Mention some of the negative interpretations of doing God's will.

Give examples:

_____

_____

4. What are some of the positive interpretations of doing God's will?

Give examples:

_____

_____

5. Prayer:

> Lord, You call us to do Your Holy will
> Things deemed impossible I dare,
> Thine is the call and Thine is the care,
> Thy wisdom shall the way prepare,
> Thy will be done.
>
> —Frederick Mann [1846–1928)

[48] Faith and the Cross

"May I never boast except in the Cross of the Lord Jesus Christ, through which the world has been crucified to me, and I to the world."

—St. Paul's Epistle to the Galatians, chapter 6:14

The good news of the Gospel is like a coin that has two sides: the cross and the glory. If we try to embrace one side while rejecting the other we falsify the Gospel. This was the mistake that St. Peter made when he rejected the mission of the suffering Christ who had to go to Jerusalem; suffer much from the religious leaders; and "be put to death" (Matthew 16:21). St. Peter's rejection of the cross was very forceful. The Gospel says that he "rebuked" Christ, stating: "God forbid it, Lord! That must never happen to you" (Matthew 16:22). The Lord corrected Peter even more forcefully: "Get behind me Satan! You are judging by man's standard, not by God's" (Matthew 16:23).

The Cross is central to the Christian faith. There is no greater symbol for Christians than the Cross: it is exalted on high, atop Christian churches; it is carried aloft during processions; it is suspended above altars of worship; it is worn around people's necks and on their clothing; and it can be seen hanging from the rear-view mirrors of cars, trucks, and busses. At baptism, children are anointed with the sign of the cross on the forehead and, when they leave this world, they are sent forth, during the burial rite, with the sign of the cross.

Why is the Cross such a dominant and central factor in our faith? The Cross is so dominant and central because it is by the sacrifice of

Christ on the cross that we have been set free from sin (Romans 6: 6) so that we can live new lives in Christ (Galatians 2: 20). When Christ was crucified on the cross, He not only atoned for our sins by His perfect sacrifice; He also enabled those who belong to Him to "have crucified the flesh with its passions and desires" (Galatians 5: 24).

The same Jesus who says: "Come to me all you who labor and are burdened, and I will refresh you" (Matthew 11:28); also says: "If anyone wants to be my disciple, he must deny himself, take up the cross and follow me" (Matthew 6:24).

How is it possible to combine joy and suffering? Does not one cancel out the other? Well, the Gospel combines both, for in pursuit of the joy of the Gospel we have to suffer; we have to deny ourselves and reject sin, which is our cross, in order to experience new life.

Today's scripture about the Cross challenges us to say no to the very attractive but one-sided worldly Gospel of instant glory; a sugar-coated Gospel that offers a false hope. There is no glory without sacrifice; there is no real joy without suffering. Jesus asked His Father in the garden to spare Him the suffering of the cross, but He submitted to the Father's will: "Not my will thine be done" (Luke 22:42).

All the countless holy men and women who have gone before us accepted the cross. Why then should it be any different for you and me? In the face of disappointment, bereavement, sickness, death of a loved one, ingratitude and failure, we need to recognize that these crosses and contradictions are the necessary condition for entering into the glorious life of Christ.

This is why St. Paul says:

"May I never boast except in the cross of the Lord Jesus Christ, through which the world has been crucified to me, and I to the world."

Reflection:

"May I never boast except in the Cross of the Lord Jesus Christ, through which the world has been crucified to me, and I to the world."

To better understand the above scriptural verse in context, you will find it helpful to read the entire passage: Galatians 6:11–18.

Please reflect on the following:

1. Why does the Gospel combine the cross and the glory?

_____

_____

2. Why did Jesus rebuke St. Peter for trying to prevent Him from accepting death on the cross?

_____

_____

3. The Cross is central to the Christian faith.

   Give examples:

_____

_____

4. Mention two main benefits for us of Christ's sacrifice on the cross.

    _____

    _____

5. How does Christ's sacrifice on the cross challenge you?

    _____

    _____

6. Prayer:

    I will not glory, nor dare I boast
    Of worldly pleasures that charm me most
    I will glory only in the Lord's true Cross
    Where new life came to those that were lost.
    If ever I stumble, if ever I fall
    God's love for me is my all.
    The blood of the Son will set me free
    From all life's burdens and misery.

    —Kirk and Deby Dearman

[49] Faith and Unity

"May they be one, so that the world will believe that
You sent Me."

—The Gospel of John, chapter 17:21

The prayer of Jesus after the last supper was that His followers be one, so that the world would know that His Father sent Him. How manifest is that message of unity among Christians in the world of today? What do we see? A Church united or a church divided? One thing is sure: the Lord wants us to be one, just as He and the Father are one. How do we achieve this unity when there is so much division and animosity among Christian denominations? Can it be done? The answer, I believe, is yes. We can be one in the essential beliefs of the faith; and we can be one in our common cause of following the example of Christ; the way, the truth, and the life.

If we are faithful to the teachings and example of Christ, Christian unity must be a top priority for us, for every Christian community or church. That is why St Paul urges the Christians of his day to "make every effort" to maintain "the unity of the spirit in the bond of peace" (Ephesians 4:3).

When St. Paul was writing, the church was still one and undivided. Yet he admonished the Christians back then to do all in their power to be as one body in Christ (Romans 12:5). The situation today is far from the unity of the early Christians. The church of Christ has suffered schisms upon schisms, divisions upon divisions, factions upon factions, with the result that anyone espousing "one flock, one shepherd" would appear to be dreaming an impossible dream. Still, that is what the Lord prayed for, and that is what we are commanded to do; to strive that all "will become one flock under one shepherd" (John 10:16).

We must all work together for Christian unity because we share so much in common. We all share in one baptism; we profess the apostle's creed; we are powered by the same Holy Spirit; we are all children of the same Father God; and we all purport to follow the example of Jesus Christ: God's only Son. What we have in common is much greater than what divides us. With this in mind, we need to come together as Christians to share the love of Christ, and to spread this good news in a world waiting to be healed.

This is a very daunting task, and I am not saying it is going to be easy. The challenge facing every Christian today in regard to Christian unity is: Can we? If we take Jesus' prayer seriously in the Gospel of John, chapter 17, the answer is quite simply: yes. Christian Unity, however, can only come about when all Christian denominations: Catholic, Protestant, and Orthodox rejoin Christ, the source and goal of any meaningful unity. It is in Christ that we will find the grace of unity. There is no other path of union among Christian denominations, Catholics, Protestants, and Orthodox, except the path that leads to conversion of hearts. The Second Vatican Council of the Catholic Church, in the Decree on Ecumenism, offers this golden rule: "There is no true ecumenism without interior conversion" (Decree Unitatis Redintegratio, 7).

We must never cease to pray and work for unity in Christ "so that the world will believe" that Jesus was sent to us by the Father (John 17:21)

Reflection:

"May they be one, so that the world will believe that You sent Me."

To better understand the above scriptural verse in context, you will find it helpful to read the entire passage: John 17:1–26.
Please reflect on the following:

1. How do we achieve the unity among Christians that Jesus prayed for at the Last Supper?

   Give examples:

   _____

   _____

2. When St. Paul wrote about Unity among Christ's followers did he face denominational divisions like we have today?

   _____

   _____

3. How can we work together to establish Christian Unity?

   Give examples:

   _____

   _____

4. What can you do, personally, to foster Christian Unity?

   Give examples:

   _____

   _____

5. Prayer (for unity):

   > Heavenly Father,
   > Gather together in the unity of one family
   > All your children dispersed by sin.
   > May your Son, Jesus,
   > Keep us in one faith and one baptism
   > Along the right path of His loving example.
   > May your Holy Spirit,
   > Bind us in the bond of peace
   > And lead us into your eternal home.

[50] Faith and Mary

"Blessed are you who believed that what was spoken to
you by the Lord would be fulfilled."

—The Gospel of Luke, chapter 1:45

When Mary heard from the angel that she was to become the mother of the Son of God, through the Holy Spirit, she was "deeply troubled." After all, she was a virgin and asked: "How, then, can this be?"

The Angel answered: "The Holy Spirit will come upon you, and God's power will rest upon you. For this reason the holy child will be called the Son of God."

The special position of Mary derives from her unique calling to be the mother of the Son of God. She was declared "full of grace" by God's messenger: that is, free from 'the fall from grace' which has been the lot of all human nature since Adam's original fall in the Garden of Eden. As the poet says, "Mary is our lowly nature's solitary boast."

In today's gospel, St. Luke presents Mary as a towering example of faith in God's Will. When informed by God's messenger that she would give birth to the Son of God, Mary immediately responded with faith: "I am the handmaid of the Lord, let it be done to me as you will."

And then, Luke tells us that "Mary set out and went as quickly as she could to visit her cousin, Elizabeth, to tell her the good news."

Elizabeth also was with child; and Mary was the first evangelist to bring the good news of Christ's birth to her.

After greeting Mary, joyfully, Elizabeth said: "Blessed are you among women and blessed is the fruit of your womb. The moment your greeting reached my ears, the child in my womb leaped with joy." That is the wonderful, spiritual effect the good news of Jesus' birth had on Elizabeth.

Mother Mary is our mother in the faith because she welcomed the Living Word of God into her life. She, more than anyone, allowed her life to be enveloped by the Living Word, meditating upon it (Luke 2:19) and giving it birth.

Mary's song of praise; the Magnificat, also foreshadows the preaching of her Son regarding the temptations of the world which stifle the life of faith. The poor and the meek, Mary sings, are God's cherished ones:

"My spirit rejoices in God my savior
for He has looked upon His lowly servant.
He has cast down the mighty from their thrones,
And He has lifted up the lowly."

Mary helps us appreciate that our whole self is never so fulfilled as when our bodies, like Mary's, become temples of the Holy Spirit.

Through the Holy Spirit, Mary gave birth to the Son of God. We, too, can give birth to the Son of God by the way we live if we let the Holy Spirit into our lives.

Reflection:

"Blessed are you who believed that what was spoken to you by the Lord would be fulfilled."

To better understand the above scriptural verse in context, you will find it helpful to read the entire scriptural passage: Luke 1:26–56.

Please reflect on the following:

1. What makes the faith of Mary so important for all Christians?

   Give examples:

   _____

   _____

2. The angel declared Mary full of Grace. How do you understand this?

   _____

   _____

3. Why was Mary the first evangelist?

   _____

   _____

4. How does Mary's faith inspire you to become a temple of the Holy Spirit, thus giving birth to her Son in your life?

_____

_____

5. Prayer:

> We sing with joy of Mary
> Whose heart with awe was stirred
> When youthful and unready
> She heard the angel's word.
> Hail Mary, full of Grace,
> The Lord is with you.
> Blessed are you among women
> And blessed is the fruit of your womb, Jesus.

ABOUT THE AUTHOR

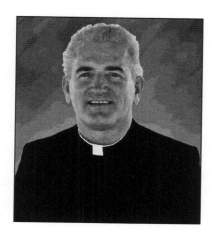

Fr. Hugh Duffy holds a Ph.D from the University of Hull, England. Born in Donegal, Ireland, he was ordained in 1966 in Dublin, Ireland. He is pastor emeritus of Sacred Heart Catholic Church, Okeechobee, Florida, where he served for thirty years and whose parishioners consisted of a multi-ethnic community of Americans, Hispanics, and Asians. Before retiring as pastor, he built a new church, debt free, for the community of Sacred Heart in 2013.

Fr. Duffy also founded Christian Community Action (CCA) in Ireland to provide a concrete way of implementing the Corporal Works of Mercy in the Gospel of Matthew, chapter 25. Thus, CCA built housing for seniors, a sheltered workshop and bakery for people with disabilities, a community center, and a treatment center for people with addictions.

Since September 2013 he has been an Outreach Speaker for Cross International, a 501(c)(3) Catholic relief and development ministry.

Fr. Duffy is the author of *Queen of the Sciences*, a book about the relationship between faith and reason in Catholic theology. A second, updated and expanded edition entitled *Faith and Reason* will be available soon. Visit www.FatherDuffy.com for more information on this and other books and videos.